Contemporary Social Philosophy

To the teachers and students of philosophy in the University of Malta, who provided the original stimulus for the material in this book

CONTEMPORARY SOCIAL PHILOSOPHY

Gordon Graham

Basil Blackwell

Copyright © Gordon Graham 1988

First published 1988

Basil Blackwell Ltd
108 Cowley Road, Oxford, OX4 1JF, UK

Basil Blackwell Inc.
432 Park Avenue South, Suite 1503
New York, NY 10016, USA

British Library Cataloguing in Publication Data

Graham, Gordon
   Contemporary social philosophy.
   1. Society — Philosophical perspectives
   I. Title
   301'.01
   ISBN 0–631–15705–0
   ISBN 0–631–15986–X Pbk

Library of Congress Cataloging in Publication Data

Graham, Gordon.
   Contemporary social philosophy/Gordon Graham.
     p.   cm.
   Bibliography: p.
   Includes index.
   ISBN 0–631–15705–0
   ISBN 0–631–15986–X (pbk.)
   1. Social sciences — Philosophy.   I. Title.
   H61.G646   1988
   300'.1–dc19

Typeset in Bembo 11 on 12.5 pt by Opus, Oxford
Printed in Great Britain by T.J. Press (Padstow) Ltd

Contents

Preface

Just what people include under the label 'social philosophy' varies a good deal. Over the last thirty-five or forty years, philosophical fashion has changed the topics that social philosophers tend to discuss. At one time their main concern was with the nature of society and the place of the individual in it – whether there is anything more to society than the people who compose it, whether human beings are essentially social. As the social sciences became more widely studied and philosophers despaired of resolving disputes between different political ideologies, philosophers found a new interest in the nature and scope of social science – is it really science, and how does it help us to understand society? Then, as moral philosophy in general underwent something of a revolution and became interested again in substantive moral issues such as abortion, euthanasia and the like, so social philosophers began to look at substantive social issues – the rights and wrongs of positive discrimination, the proper way to provide medical care, and so on.

This book aims to introduce newcomers to all these different aspects of social philosophy, but in fact the variety is not as great as it might seem. Indeed, part of the purpose of the book is just to show that behind the different trends and fashions there is a great deal of continuity, and that all these topics are closely related to recurring themes and conceptions.

The book is introductory, but this does not mean it is elementary. The aim is to help readers to get to grips with the real and important issues of social philosophy and to start to think about them for themselves. One way to do this would be to set out the ideas of great thinkers past and present, but a better way, in my view, is to present lively and topical arguments with which the reader can engage directly.

This second method, however, has the disadvantage that it

may more easily be misunderstood. Since arguments must reach conclusions on the issues they address, in places it will appear that the book takes sides in a way that an introduction should not. So it needs to be stressed at the outset that, despite appearances to the contrary sometimes, the purpose of this book is to get the reader started on the arguments, not to settle all the issues.

The second feature to which attention must be drawn, since it too can be misunderstood, is the relative simplicity of some of the presentation. Where space is limited decisions have to be made, not just about which subjects to leave out (and some interesting topics have been omitted), but about how much to write on those that are included. Inevitably, where the introduction takes the form of an argument, this means that decisions have to be made about when an argument should stop, and so conclusions are arrived at even when it is evident to those who know the subject well that further replies and counter-replies could be made. So once again it must be stressed that the arguments presented here are not to be thought of as final in any sense.

What is essential to introducing philosophy in this way is that the line of argument should be clear and well informed. This is especially true of social philosophy, because nearly all the topics it discusses are of interest to other branches of social study. Consequently, it is highly desirable to make clear to students of subjects other than philosophy – politics, sociology, economics and social work theory, for instance – just what sort of contribution it is that philosophy can make, and for this reason an introduction must avoid specialist language even more than is usually desirable. On this front I have made a special effort and I hope, therefore, that students of these other disciplines will find the book interesting and useful.

Chapters 1, 2 and 3 are the longest and provide the theoretical background against which specific social issues are discussed in subsequent chapters. The final chapter discusses another range of important topics, raised by the main arguments of the book.

I am grateful to my colleague Christopher Bryant for invaluable help with the word processor.

Gordon Graham
St Andrews

1

What is Society?

The word 'society' may be used in a host of different ways. The most uncontroversial uses refer to groups of people who get together for some shared professional or recreational purpose – for example, the Society of Motor Manufacturers or the Society of Friends. But when we speak of 'society' in general we normally mean something larger and more important than any of these other societies, something with a public and usually a political character. It is society in this sense which is invoked, for instance, when references are made to people's 'paying their debt to society', an idea which calls up all the highly public institutions of legal punishment – police, courts and prisons. Similarly it is in this very general sense that society is said to do or have failed to have done a wide variety of different things – to determine the relative status and opportunities of individuals and to have duties and obligations towards them, usually in matters of health or education or some other sort of welfare provision.

But what exactly is this 'society' to which debts are owed and upon which responsibilities are so frequently placed? One response to this question which occurs quickly to many people identifies 'society' with 'the government'. But we need not think long about this answer before we see that it will not do. To begin with, governments come and go, they can be elected and replaced, can have support or lack it. None of these things is true about society. Certainly, a society can change, but not by election or appointment, and it is only very rarely that we can date the beginning or end of a society. In the second place, when people argue that society has a duty to provide every child with a decent education, say, and call upon the government of the day to recognize this duty in legislative terms, they do not mean to suggest that it is only the government of the day which has that obligation, or that the legislation initiated should bind only that government. They mean, of course, that such provision should be made during the rule of any and every government.

We could put the same thing another way by saying that a decent minimum of education should be included in the provisions made by the *state*. This might lead us to think that 'state' and 'society' mean pretty much the same thing. If so, the philosophy of society is really the philosophy of the state (which is the same as saying that social philosophy is really political philosophy). But once again, as soon as we think about it, we can see fairly readily that society and the state are *not* the same thing.

In the first place, within a society the state is only one institution amongst many others and may easily be distinguished from industrial companies, banks, churches, universities, football clubs and so on. Of course in most parts of the modern world the state is by far the largest and in many ways the most important social institution. It generally employs large numbers of people, and in some places a majority of the workforce. But it never employs *everyone*. Soldiers, police, judges, tax inspectors and customs men are obviously officers of the state, and there are also a great many clerks, mechanics, cooks and so on, who, if not exactly *officers* of the state, are nevertheless parts of its administrative apparatus. But usually there are also a great many people in these occupations who are not state employees; some occupations – shopkeeping for instance – are hardly represented in the organization of the state; and always there are those who cannot be employees of the state, because they have no paid occupation at all – infants, housewives, the aged or the nomadic. They are still members of society, however, even though they are not parts of the administrative apparatus of the state, and from this we can conclude that state and society are not identical.

Of course, these people are, usually, *subject to* the state – they must obey its laws and edicts – but this does not mean that they are *constituent parts* of it. They need not even be citizens. Foreigners and *Gastarbeiter* (those who have work permits but no right to vote in elections and so on), unlike diplomats, are subject to the laws of the state in which they reside, even when they are not citizens of that state but of some other. Conversely, we should remember that anthropologists quite properly describe different nomadic tribes as forming distinctive societies of their own, and many such tribes may come under the control of a single state. This is the case, in point of fact, for many of the tribes of East Africa, tribes which have existed as distinct societies for centuries, but have only recently come within the control of a state. And from this it follows once more that state and society cannot be one and the same thing.

Enough should now have been said to show how social philosophy begins, and indeed, how necessary it is. 'Society', 'government', 'state' and 'nation' are words in regular use, not only in newspapers and on television but also in the conversations of most people. Yet, once we begin to think about the sort of remarks people commonly make, we will all be aware of a striking need for clarification. It is for this reason that social philosophy must begin by drawing some distinctions. It would be wrong, however, to suppose that this means we must begin by 'defining our terms'. It is often thought that because most of the moral, social and political matters with which philosophers concern themselves are highly contentious, the best way to begin is by offering definitions of the words that will be used. But this is really quite pointless. If the definition that is offered is uncontentious, this will only be because it is sufficiently vague to span the differences between those in dispute, in which case it can settle none of the interesting questions. Or else it will be precise enough to settle some of the issues (usually in favour of those who offer it), but only by having built into it answers to the questions on which the disputants are divided. If the first of these is true, the definition is unhelpful; if the second, it is merely stipulative, and there is no reason why anyone should abide by someone else's stipulations.

Definitions, then, are worthless, but we still need to be clear on what we are talking about. What we need are not so much definitions as distinctions. Distinctions, unlike definitions, can remain fuzzy at the edges, so long as we can see at least *some* clear and central applications of them. So let us try distinguishing between government, state, and society.

Government

Governments are, relative to the societies they govern, quite small groups of people. Generally a government is formed from only a minority of the parties of people that work to have them elected. Indeed a government may well constitute only a small minority, or even none, of those who are popularly elected as representatives. So, for instance, only a few members of the majority party in the British House of Commons will be members of the government, and in the United States no elected member of Congress can belong to the executive branch of government. Governments come and go. They are, in the main and in relation to the societies they govern, fairly short-lived. In many countries the constitution places a time limit on the life of any one government. This seems not only intelligible, but sensible, whereas it would be absurd to attempt to put a constitutional time limit on the existence of a society. We may say, then, that a government is the set of people which rules a society, and it does so through the apparatus of the state.

State

Unlike that of a government the life of a state cannot be constitutionally limited. States do go out of existence, but they do so through war, conquest, famine, disease or natural disaster, not legislative fiat. A government *uses* and controls the state: it is not identical with it. But we must also distinguish the state from the society of which it is a part. In fact, societies can exist without states. Many have done so in the past and some, commonly nomadic tribes, still do. A state is, roughly, a self-consciously organized institution by means of which a society is regulated and preserved. Nomadic tribes do have means by which their societies are governed – life in them is not a matter of constant chaos – but they need have nothing resembling a state: no legislature, formal judiciary, standing army, tax collection system and so on. The nation-state, with its clearly defined sovereign territory, which nowadays we are inclined to think characteristic of society as such, is a relatively recent phenomenon. Though it is true that complex forms of organized administration for the government of public affairs can be found very far back in the history of mankind (the Babylonian empire, for instance, had a highly sophisticated administration), it is also true that until recently these were the exception rather than the rule.

Usually the state claims for itself a monopoly of the legitimate use of coercive force, which is a way of saying that the officers of the state (army, police, prison guards, militia and so on) are the only people who may properly employ force in ensuring that other people comply with their commands. This is a feature of the state which some philosophers and political theorists have thought to be its peculiar and distinguishing characteristic. It is, after all, the idea of *legitimate* coercion which distinguishes the police from the Mafia. Without legitimacy, the state appears no better than a more permanent and perhaps somewhat more civilized equivalent of the marauding robber barons of the past. But there are difficulties in taking legitimate coercion to be the defining characteristic of states. First, there seems no *logical* reason why a state should not permit self-defence or citizen's arrest: many do. Where these things are permitted people who are not officers of the state may properly use force on occasion, and from this it follows that the state is *not* the monopolist of legitimate force. Secondly, questions and even doubts can be raised about the basis of legitimacy which this definition assumes. In saying that the state is the sole legitimate user of coercive force, we can hardly mean that the state is the monopolist of *legally* permitted coercion, because this would make the characterization trivially true, since the state makes the laws. But if we mean that its use of force is *morally* legitimate, we face the objections both of those who believe that no force whatever is morally legitimate and of those who think that on occasion an individual may be morally justified in using force, even against the state. Finally, modern states engage in many activities where their coercive powers cannot properly be used. The state might run a system of hospitals, for instance, but it does not follow from the fact that they are state-run that citizens can legitimately be coerced into using them.

For these reasons, amongst others, it does not seem right to characterize the state in terms of force. Let us agree, then, to describe states as the administrative institutions by which (some) societies are governed. This is somewhat vaguer than the characterization we have rejected, but since it does not purport to be an exhaustive definition, only a general description that will allow us to distinguish states from governments, it can still provide sufficient clarity for a profitable discussion of many of the most interesting questions of social philosophy to begin.

Society

If the state is an institution, society plainly is not. It has no constitution, no budget, no personnel. Rather than being some one thing, indeed, it seems to be more of an umbrella, a catch-all by which we refer to a plethora of individuals and organizations – businesses, churches, schools, clubs, charities, councils, lawcourts, prisons and so on, which we believe stand in some relation to each other, even if we don't quite know what that relation is. But even this is not certain, because it is not at all clear where the boundaries between societies are to be drawn, at least in the way that it is usually clear where the boundaries between different states lie. People quite readily speak of British, French or American society, which suggests boundaries of a vaguely political sort, but they speak just as readily of Western society, which has cultural as well as political overtones, and seems to imply that one society is able to contain many others. These various ways of talking leave it unclear whether we should think of the concept of 'society' primarily in political terms, that is to say alongside the concepts of 'state', 'government' and so on, or whether we should think of it chiefly as having a place alongside concepts like 'language' and 'culture'.

These and other related questions are the stock in trade of social philosophy. This is because they admit of no easy or straightforward answers, but can be answered only by extended thought and argument. Indeed it is not really correct to say that they can be answered at all. Rather, in response to the question 'What is a society?' we can offer arguments and considerations which will, if we pursue them properly, lead to an understanding of the range and complexity of the issues that such a question raises.

Conceptions of society

In fact, as we will see, the question 'What is a society?' is somewhat misleading. It suggests an inquiry into some matter of fact – social facts or facts about concepts – whereas what is needed is *normative* inquiry. That is to say, the proper question which lies at the heart of social philosophy is not really a question about how things are but about how we ought to think about them, not what a society is so much as how it ought to be conceived. We could mark this difference by saying that there is no one discoverable *concept* of society, only a variety of competing *conceptions*. And faced with this variety, social philosophy is just the inquiry which asks 'Which conception of society have I most reason to employ?'.

Social philosophy, then, is a normative or evaluative inquiry, but this does not mean that it has no interest in matters of fact, no place for the observation of social realities or the careful delineation of concepts as they are used. On the contrary, since the competing conceptions of society between which social philosophy attempts to adjudicate make many appeals to facts of one sort or another, factual argument must play an important part in social philosophy. But the facts are not important on their own. Rather, which facts we need to know and how much of what we already know is relevant to thinking about society, has to be established by an overall concern with social and moral *values*. For instance, different conceptions of society carry different recommendations for social policy, and the plausibility of these recommendations will depend in part upon what social inquiry tells us are possible ways for human beings to live together. A policy which, if it is to be successful, requires *saintliness* amongst those to whom it applies, will be defective just on the grounds that human beings are *not* saints. Social philosophy, then, must be *well informed*.

Nevertheless, the truly evaluative nature of the subject will be apparent as we turn from theoretical questions about the nature of society to questions about the desirability of different forms of social organization, and the values those different social forms seek to realize. But to begin the argument we must first set out, in a largely schematic way, the various conceptions of society in terms of which these facts and policies are to be understood.

Of the many conceptions of society that have been advanced in the history of human thought, two are specially important, because they have influenced the course of social theory, social policy and political debate more than any other. Moreover, though they themselves admit of variation, together they underlie almost all the major political programmes of the modern world. These two conceptions are called by a variety of names. Amongst the commonest are 'individualism', 'social atomism', 'communitarianism' and 'collectivism'. I shall use the terms 'individualism' and 'communitarianism' in order to avoid some of the associations that 'atomism' and 'collectivism' now have. Labels, however, are not important in themselves, and there need be no confusion over different uses so long as we are clear about just which ideas are being referred to. In any case, the two conceptions of society with which we are concerned are best thought of as clusters of ideas, rather than precisely formulated theories.

Individualism

At the heart of individualism is the view that in social philosophy, political theory and practice, in moral thought and action, it is individual human beings who must, in some sense, be regarded as prior to society. In just what sense the individual is to be thought primary is one of the main topics to be discussed in this book, but whatever we take the best version of this claim to be, it carries with it an implied view of society, namely that society is a sort of *association*. An association in this sense is a group that we join, usually, though not necessarily, for our mutual benefit. Most associations are voluntary – we belong to them only because and so long as we choose to – but more importantly, perhaps, they are organizations which are constituted, criticized, reformed, and occasionally abolished according to their ability to satisfy the interests and purposes of their members. In short, they are *for* the people who belong to them. So, for instance, a stamp club, which, because of the way it was organized, actually *prevented* its members from collecting stamps satisfactorily, would unquestionably require reform, because we can see straight away that something has gone wrong when a club or association of this limited sort appears to be being run for its own sake rather than for the sake of the people who belong to it.

Society, of course, could not be quite like any other association. To begin with it seems implausible to suppose that it is voluntary – how could we set about leaving? We could leave one society, it seems, only to find ourselves, willy-nilly, in some other. The most determined hermits will belong to some society or other at some point in their lives. This is, perhaps, what most people mean when they say 'Man is a social animal'. They mean that human beings are always members of some society or other, rather than that they are by nature *sociable*, that is, fond of being in the company of others. Whether membership of society is in the strongest sense necessary for human beings, and therefore not a voluntary matter, is a question we shall be asking in due course, but on the surface, there is at least this striking difference between society at large and any other club or association.

John Locke

Still, this fact does not prevent us from thinking of society as primarily an association, and if we do, this will have implications for how we think about the state. Many of these implications are made plain in one of the first and most obviously individualist theories to be formulated explicitly, namely John Locke's theory in his *Second Treatise of Government*. Locke was an English philosopher writing around the time of the Glorious Revolution of 1688. To understand his political thought, two features of this revolution are worth noting. First, the king and queen who ascended the throne following the deposition of James II, William and Mary, had no real legal right to do so. They were merely offered the crown by representatives of Parliament, which is to say, in a sense, by representatives of the people. Secondly, the revolution resulted, among other things, in a Bill of Rights, which gave individual citizens certain protective rights against their political masters. On Locke's view of society, this is just how things should be, since an organized society, as opposed to the natural societies which animals form and which primeval people may have formed, is an association called into existence precisely to serve the purposes of those who join it. Consequently, the state should be thought of as the management structure of a society and judged accordingly, by its efficiency and success.

Locke may well have been the most articulate spokesman of the individualist conception of society rather than its originator, but so influential has that conception been that it is hard for us to appreciate the radical revolution in thought which in its day it constituted. Hitherto, subjects had been regarded as servants of their rulers, and the relation between subject and monarch was thought personal rather than legal, more like the relation of child to parent, say, than the relation between employer and employee. It was this personal conception that Locke attacked in his *First Treatise*, a critique of Sir Robert Filmer's *Patriarcha* which advocated the conception of the monarch as father of his people. But with the idea of the people *choosing* their own rulers and having legal rights against them came the belief that it is the rulers who are servants of the people rather than the other way about, and that the relation between them is a contractual one, based on a *social* contract, just as other relations are based on *legal* contracts.

The limited state

Now if we think of social and political relationships in this way it will become apparent immediately that we can accept only some conceptions of the state, namely conceptions of a *limited* state. For, if the nature of society is to help each of us go about our own business, the state must be thought of as merely an instrument for the more efficient functioning of society, something whose constitution and conduct cannot be a law unto itself, but must be scrutinized, corrected and even resisted, in the light of its usefulness to the purposes of its citizens. On this conception, then, there are things that the state cannot do and rights which individuals possess independently of the legal system under which they live – natural rather than legal rights – by which loyalty to the state is bounded.

Of course, even if we accept this conception of society and with it a belief in the limited state, we have not accepted any account of just how far the state should be limited. Those who accept the individualist conception of society may differ, and have indeed traditionally differed very widely, on what it allows the state to do. Some are minimalists, like the American philosopher Robert Nozick, whose book *Anarchy, State, and Utopia* makes extensive use of Locke's conception, and they believe that many of the activities of the state with which we are familiar, and which for the most part we accept happily enough, are quite unjustifiable – if, that is, we accept that society is an association of individuals with rights. Many others, on the other hand, who are liberal individualists in the sense that they think of society as an association of free individuals, are happy to accept a wide range of state activities, because they think that these can be explained and understood as promoting the interests and liberties of the individual.

It will be an important part of this book to explore these questions, and to try to decide, in the light of the most satisfactory conception of society, just what we are entitled to expect the state to do; but before going further along this path, it is necessary to outline the second main, and alternative, conception of society, that of the communitarian or holist.

Communitarianism

Individualism views society as a specially constructed device, an arrangement intended and designed to serve the independent purposes of its members, in the way that a bank or building society is meant to serve the interests of its customers. In other words, there is nothing natural or necessary about society, or about the state, in the way that there is something natural about the family. Both society and the state are, in older language, *artifices*. The force of this idea lies in its implications. If society is an artificial construct, something like a university perhaps, then its organization will be controlled, and the judgements we pass upon it will be determined, according to the desires and self-chosen purposes of individuals that they have outside or independently of their society. Hence the name 'individualism'. Secondly, to explain the value of social membership and to justify the coercive actions of the state, we will have to make appeal to those individual desires and purposes. For individualism, society has no higher purpose of its own, and there is no grander social or political scheme of things in which individuals must learn to play their part, for society's greater good or glory. In individualism, each autonomous adult human being is, literally, king, and other 'kings' take such authority as they possess from, and only on the will of, the individuals they rule.

In short, on the liberal individualist view society is necessarily and essentially a plurality, a mere association of different views and interests. This way of putting it enables us to make the sharpest possible contrast with its principal rival – communitarianism – which regards society as a community, and this, as the very word implies, means that society is in some way a *unity*, a single thing in which individual members are bound together. The view of society as a community underlies at least two very different political philosophies. Whereas individualism is associated chiefly with political liberalism of various sorts, the conception of society as community is to be found underlying political ideologies of left and right. Its first expression is to be found in Plato's *Republic*, a book written about 2400 years ago, and Plato's social theory has strong affinities with twentieth-century Fascism and with some varieties of conservatism. On the other hand, the belief that society is a community is also to be found, more and less explicitly, in most non-Marxist versions of socialism, and the idea of putting the interests of community before those of the individual often underlies socialist political policies. Between political philosophies of the left and right, of course, there are a great many important differences, but however significant these may be, there is at least this much agreement between them – that society is a community and not merely an association of distinct individuals – and it is one which explains in part their combined opposition to liberal individualism.

But the measure of agreement should not be exaggerated. The *way* in which each conceives society to be a community is notably different. One method of bringing out this difference is to compare the different analogies that, traditionally, each has employed.

Society as a body politic

We speak of *members* of society. The language of membership has its home in anatomy, where different parts of the body are described as members in order to signify that they comprise a composite whole. So too, many political theorists, chiefly in what we now think of as right-wing traditions, have spoken of society as an 'organism'. The force of the metaphor is this. An arm is different from a leg. Each has its distinctive character and function, but both have any character or function at all only as parts of a body, in which each has a distinctive but subservient place. Thus, just as it would be absurd to suppose that the health of the body is to be judged entirely by the health of the arm, or the leg, so too it is absurd to judge the 'health' of society solely by the well-being of its members. Of course, the health of the body is not to be thought of as something over and above the health of its members, but this does not alter the fact that it is only *as parts of* the body, and not as individual members, that the health of arms, eyes, legs and so on is important. This is demonstrated by the fact that in certain circumstances it may be right and sensible to sacrifice an arm or an eye for the health of the body as a whole, and so too it may be that circumstances require the sacrifice of some members of society for the good of the whole.

Just how far the metaphor of society as an organism is to be pressed is a highly contentious matter. Plato thought it obvious that, just as the head must rule the other parts of the body for the sake of the body as a whole, including those other parts, so society must have a 'natural' ruler. But not all theorists who have been persuaded of the aptness of this metaphor have pressed it home to this conclusion, though all modern Fascist movements have stressed the need of a Leader (Duce, *Führer*, Caudillo, etc.) Others, like the eighteenth-century British parliamentarian and conservative thinker Edmund Burke, have sought the 'head' of the body politic in something much less tangible, namely its constitution and traditions, which are not just to be obeyed, but reverenced.

The metaphor of the organic society has led, in political thinking, to emphasis upon the virtues of order and continuity, and aversion to radical change, because radical political change, on this view, is comparable to injuring a biological organism, in ignorance and with a foolish disregard for its susceptible physiological nature. Order and continuity are hardly the values we associate with the political left, however, and so it is not surprising that the anatomical metaphor for the social community has not found favour among socialists. But the idea of a community, in opposition to liberal individualism, is still there. The difference is that their preferred analogy, if there is one, is with the family.

Society as a family

Consider a family. It is not properly to be thought of as a mere association of individuals met together for purposes which they happen to have in common. We are born into our families, and however much we like or dislike the fact, this is something we cannot alter. I shall always remain someone's son, and someone else's father. Even death cannot undo these facts. What binds us to this one set of people rather than some other is not community of purpose but, ideally at any rate, community of *feeling*. Of course, we have interests and occupations outside our family, and when our family functions well it will assist us in these, but we should not suppose that its value lies solely in the contribution it can make in this connection. Rather, the family itself has a claim upon us. We are by nature family-forming creatures, and moreover we are ourselves in large part *formed by* our families. Family relations can never be annihilated, though they may, for all practical purposes, be sundered by envy, hatred or plain indifference. Conversely, they will flourish under a regime of respect, affection, tolerance and care. And what this shows is that the family is a natural formation, not an artificial device.

So too with society, according to the socialist. The liberal individualist who wants us to think of society as an artifice, useful for our own antecedently chosen purposes, is like a man who judges the worth of his family only in the light of its usefulness to him. He has neither affection for nor pride in it. He has, in short, no sense of belonging. But in this he is doubly mistaken. For, on the socialist view, we just are naturally social creatures, as we are family creatures, and further, there is good reason to regard social ties as valuable in themselves. This is why socialists have stressed (in addition to the liberty and equality on the value of which liberals will generally concur), the political virtue of *fraternity*, or, if a less familial term is desirable, *comradeship*.

Of course, socialists, even if they *do* speak of the brotherhood of all men, do not think that society *is* a family. Societies are *sui generis*, that is, they are a special kind of thing which has no direct counterpart elsewhere. Similarly, the Platonists (to give a useful label to the alternative right-wing conception of social community) do not think that society *is* a body. Both analogies are intended only to point up the essential unity of society, and hence the inappropriateness of the artificial, almost mechanical conception of the liberal individualist. Sometimes it is important to know just how far metaphors like these are meant to be pressed, but at any rate enough has been said to show that, ranged against the individualist view of society as an association, a piece of machinery for the advancement of individual purposes, is the communitarian conception, which may take either of two forms: one which compares it to an organism, something that is not to be equated just with the sum of its parts and which may flourish, sicken or die independently of any of its parts; and the other which views it as something like a family, held together by ties of loyalty and affection, and with a value beyond the purposes of the individual. The next step is to ask about the implications of each.

If we think of society along the lines of the organic analogy, we will tend to think of social programmes and policies in a vaguely medical way. So, the good or ill of society will be a matter of 'treating' it correctly, and this in turn will be a matter of respecting the natural divisions and the natural hierarchies within it. Hence the organic conception often generates, as its history confirms, a cautious and somewhat mysterious approach to social policy, which is informed not so much by general principles or an eye to consequences of a clearly estimable sort, as by a preference for 'natural leaders', who will, in the words of one famous twentieth-century conservative theorist, Michael Oakeshott, 'pursue the intimations' of the political tradition in which they find themselves.

Alternatively, the conception of society as a community of *comrades* will generate social policies which are informed first and foremost by moral principle. It is this conception which can give the clearest idea of what a 'good' society would be, just as we can give a pretty clear sense to the idea of what a good family is like. The good society, like the good family, will be one in which everyone is equally important and where, rather than each individual being left to fend for him or herself, the strengths of some will be drawn upon to assist the weaknesses of others. The individualist's conception of society is one in which there is nothing especially bad about the weakest going to the wall, nothing worse, at any rate, than there is about the slowest runner losing the race. But on the socialist's conception, to allow the weakest to go to the wall in society is just like allowing the weakest of one's children to suffer and die, and to do so for no better reason than that they are weak. In a morally admirable family, an individual's weakness is a reason for giving *greater* care and attention, not less, and so it is in a morally admirable society.

The communitarian state

On both communitarian views there is no theoretical or principled limit on what the state, in the name of society, may and may not do. Individualism, it will be recalled, gives moral priority to members of society as individuals, and it marks this priority by according them non-legal or natural rights, which means on the one hand that there are things the state cannot do to them, even in the interests of society as a whole, and on the other that their obligations to the state and to society are limited. Communitarianism, by contrast, gives no such priority to the individual. It need not give moral priority to society either (though Fascist versions generally have done), but the fact that it conceives society as a moral community beyond the individual means that *any* action by the state on behalf of society could in principle be morally permissible, and even morally obligatory.

It is very important, however, not to confuse an *unlimited* state with a *totalitarian* one. To say that some state or other is unlimited is to make a remark about the possible rather than the actual range of its activities in the society it controls. A state may be unlimited without taking a large and positive role in every aspect of life; it is sufficient, for it to be unlimited, that it *may* take part in any aspect of life. The difference between the unlimited and the totalitarian state is the difference between Britain and the Soviet Union. The British political system, though it has liberal elements and is one of the least oppressive regimes in the world, is nonetheless one in which the state is unlimited, because the state in Britain may lawfully take an interest in any aspect of social and individual life whatever. In addition to the prevention of crime, enforcement of contracts and defence of the realm it may, and does, take part in commercial enterprises, run or grant monopolies, control the watching of television by licence, and decide the hours during which alcohol (and other goods) may be bought and sold, what films may be watched and books published, and even what prayers may be said in the public worship of the Church of England.

If, however, the state is a *limited* one, there are things it cannot constitutionally do. Examples are not so easy to find because there are very few limited states. Not surprisingly, given the influence of Locke's writings on its founding fathers, the United States is one of them. Even here the limitations are not so very numerous and do not include several that should be close to the true individualist's heart, but amongst those that there are is the complete separation of church and state, for the law may not be used in any way to assist or promote (as opposed to permit) religious activity. And this restriction is there for a principled reason – namely the protection of the individual's inviolable right to freedom of worship.

However, just as an unlimited state need not be totalitarian, so a limited state may use its powers in a heavy-handed and divisive way. The respective merits of the two, therefore, are not to be assessed in terms of their character as experienced by those who live under them, but rather according to the acceptability of the ideas that they embody. It is to these that we now turn.

Individualism versus communitarianism

If individualism and communitarianism are not straightforward descriptive theories of what society is, how are we to judge between them? To call these alternative *conceptions* of society is partly a way of underlining the fact that the difference between them is not as simple as the difference between, for instance, two theories of how a crime was committed. Consequently no simple appeal to the facts that sociology or history might uncover is likely to settle this dispute.

Some people have thought that this means that such a fundamental dispute cannot be settled at all, but this is too gloomy a view to take. Not all disputes are disputes about matters of fact – we can also dispute about which film we ought to go to or which books are worth reading, for instance – and if these disputes are to be settled rationally there must be other ways of deciding differences of opinion than straightforward appeal to 'the facts'.

In the case of the competing conceptions of individualism and communitarianism there are indeed alternative strategies open to us. The first of these is to look at the arguments that proponents and opponents of the different positions have brought for and against them, and to consider who has the best of the argument. The second is to explore the implications of each for social policy, as best we can, and to rely upon deeply held convictions about what is and what is not desirable to judge the acceptability of these implications and thus the acceptability of the conceptions of society from which they spring. Of course, the deeply held convictions to which we appeal are not wholly independent of the beliefs we have about the truth or cogency of different views of society, so that there is and must be some interplay between what just strikes us as plainly right or wrong and what the various arguments tell us we ought to regard as right and wrong. For this reason, nothing in this area admits of wholly *conclusive* argument (very few areas of human thought do, including most natural science), but we can at least hope to arrive at what the twentieth-century American philosopher John Rawls, in his book *A Theory of Justice*, has called a 'reflective equilibrium', that is, a reasonable balance between our arguments and our pre-reflective convictions, so that they hang together in a fairly cogent and coherent way.

In the next chapter I shall proceed in the first of these ways, by considering one of the most fundamental disputes between individualism and its critics, namely the possible relations between the individual and society. In subsequent chapters I shall adopt the second strategy and see what the implications of each is for the actual running of society, and whether or not these are acceptable. But before that we must pause to consider the arguments of a different type of critic, one who claims that the dispute we are about to engage in and the arguments we are about to consider are, on both sides, utterly misguided: in other words, that social philosophy, as I have outlined it here, is a waste of time. Of these critics two are very famous – Marx and Machiavelli.

TWO ALTERNATIVES: MARX AND MACHIAVELLI

Marx

Karl Marx was a nineteenth-century German political and social thinker. His name has become one of the best known in the history of the world and somewhere in the region of half the people on the globe live in countries which officially hail him as their constitutional inspiration. Nevertheless, few politicians or other people who are avowedly Marxist have any real understanding of his writings, though given their volume and density this is hardly surprising.

Marx began his studies with an interest in philosophy, but he came to the view that philosophy is not the right way of tackling social questions. Consequently, he moved on to social theory of a rather more general sort, and drew upon the writings of French socialists and English economists as well as the philosophy of the most influential German thinker of his day, G.W.F. Hegel. The resulting theory altered Hegelian philosophy out of all recognition as Marx himself acknowledged when, in the preface to the first volume of his most famous work *Capital*, he claimed to have 'turned Hegel on his head'.

The principal feature of this revolution in ideas was its rejection of pure philosophical inquiry. It would be very odd, therefore, if we were able to include Marx as a direct contributor to the discussion of social philosophy, since he thought philosophy an idle inquiry. His belief was that the abstract examination of social, political and legal ideas fails to take account of the actual practical circumstances in which they have grown up and in which they must be advanced and commended. Consequently, social philosophy, even if it comes

up with 'good' ideas, is no better from a practical point of view
than Utopian dreaming. Such dreams, however attractive, do
nothing to assist in the active transformation of society in the
direction to which they aspire. They are, as we say, 'idealistic',
and in place of this sort of philosophy what is needed, according
to Marx, is a historical science, a rigorous and theoretically well
conceived understanding of historical processes and forces.
Such a science is what Marx (and others) thought he had
developed (which is why Engels, Marx's lifelong associate,
made a comparison between Marx and Darwin in his oration at
Marx's graveside), and it is the promise of this that continues to
stimulate academic interest in his writings today.

According to Marx, society has developed as a result of two
forces – the need for people to provide themselves with the
means of survival and the steady growth in population. Given
these forces, people in society will form what we might call
'systems of production' by which they exploit the natural
resources that surround them for their mutual benefit.
However, as the population grows the demands on the system
of production which has developed also grow, until in fact the
system cannot meet all those needs. Faced with such circumstances those whose basic needs are *not* being met have no
alternative but to abandon the existing system in favour of some
other, and this is what is happening during periods of great
social and economic change. Of course, those whose needs *are*
adequately met under the old system have no reason to abandon
it and will want to preserve it. Consequently, any society will
have two classes, one which favours the existing system of
production, and one which is compelled by necessity to
overthrow it. Economic systems are dynamic, however, which
is to say that they are perpetually undergoing change. In Marx's
theory social and political changes are to be understood as
institutional results of the struggle between those who see their
survival as depending upon the existing economic system and
those who perceive that *their* survival depends upon the demise
of that very system.

This method of analysis is quite general but Marx was
primarily concerned to investigate the economic and social
history of Western Europe, to analyse its present condition with
a view to discovering the most likely course of the future, and

his conclusion was very striking. Marx thought that not only would the present economic system – capitalism – very soon come to an end, but that with it would come the end of the interplay of forces that had determined all previous history. In short there would come into existence a *classless* society.

The reason for this lies with the nature of capitalism. To simplify a very complex matter we can say that as a system of production capitalism has two main features. First, unlike any previously existing system it can produce an *infinite* quantity of goods. This means that one of the forces of social change has in fact been ended in capitalism – namely the driving need for an increase in production to accommodate increased demand. However, the fact that capitalism can produce an infinite quantity of goods does not mean that infinitely many needs are met under this system. On the contrary, despite its productive capacity, capitalism progressively satisfies fewer and fewer needs. This is, in fact, what is sometimes called the contradiction in capital and it arises from the inner workings of an economic system under which the distribution of wealth is highly unequal between capitalists and workers. As a result, though vast quantities of goods can be produced, larger and larger numbers of people are drawn into the labouring classes which, as wages fall, are less and less able to buy the goods. Consequently, these people are just as unable to satisfy the basic needs for survival as they were under older systems, in which the necessary quantities of goods could *not* be produced. Thus, as with those other systems, capitalism produces its revolutionary class, the class whose best interests are served by the collapse of the system. Moreover, again as a result of the inner working of capitalism, this class grows ever larger while the ruling class – those whose interests are best served by the preservation of capitalism – shrinks accordingly, from which it follows, Marx thought, that the demise of capitalism is inevitable.

But the demise of capitalism does not signal the end of industrialization. Those who thought that the poverty and the degradation of the labouring classes in the nineteenth century were a result of the advent of towns and factories, and who looked back with nostalgia to an agricultural and pastoral past, were the objects of some of Marx's bitterest scorn, since in his view they wholly failed to grasp the march of history. Rather, the demise of capitalism signals the end of a certain financial and legal system under which the means of producing goods are privately owned. For, once the means of production are *publicly* owned, the problem of unequal distribution which private ownership created will be solved, and the creative potential of capitalism will be released fully. Thus *everyone's* needs will be adequately met and no one, consequently, will have an interest in the destruction of the system of production that will ensue. There will, in short, be no classes.

In such a world, freed from economic necessity, people will begin to make true history. Social and political events, that is to say, will be as people mean them to be, and not as economic necessity dictates. At that time, critical speculation on different social forms and principles will be in order because it will then be possible to fashion the social world as we will. But before then, in a world which is still held in the thraldom of labouring for survival, such speculation is pointless, or worse than pointless since it distracts us from the proper understanding of the historical process and from the practical task of easing the birth pangs of the new era (as Marx himself puts it).

This is a very simple outline of Marx's view, but it should be sufficient to show why a Marxist might think the sort of social philosophy which this book aims to introduce is worthless. Whether Marx's view carries this implication depends on whether or not we can say that the capitalist system as described and analysed has ceased to exist, for if it has any restrictions its existence may have imposed will have been lifted. Most Marxists seem to believe that capitalism is still with us and that the classless society has yet to arrive. But there is good reason to think that in its essentials the economic system of Western Europe *has* changed radically since Marx's time, and that private ownership of the means of production, as Marx conceived it, is almost nonexistent.

There are three important phenomena to be recorded. In the first place widespread state ownership of major utilities, key areas of manufacture and financial institutions has brought these out of the control of private capitalists. This may be for good or ill, but the fact remains that there are sizeable sections of the means of production in most modern states that are not privately owned. Secondly, contrary to Marx's predictions, private ownership of capital is now very widely disseminated, because through the investments of insurance and pension schemes almost everyone in a modern Western democracy has some stake in, and derives some benefit from, capital. This form of dissemination is very important.It is in effect *public* ownership that is not state ownership, and it divorces the ownership of capital from its *control*. For the most part the means of production are no longer controlled by those who own them but by a managerial class which plays no part in Marx's analysis. Thirdly, since the late nineteenth century, redistributive taxation systems have directed purchasing power to those who have been incapable of earning it within the productive system. Whatever its merits or demerits, this has been an institutional solution to the contradiction of capitalism not envisaged by Marx.

There is reason, then, to doubt whether capitalism remains and therefore whether the pointlessness which Marx saw in the writings of the German philosophers of his day also holds true of modern social philosophy. But in any case, his strictures are convincing only if his theory is sound. For my part I do not believe that it is, though the space it would need to show this prevents my offering a demonstration of it here. It is sufficient, in fact, to point out that, even under conditions of capitalism, or any other class-structured system, we need not be unduly impressed by the usefulness or otherwise of our subject. In a very famous sentence (one of eleven theses on the German philosopher Feuerbach) Marx claimed that 'The philosophers have only *interpreted* the world, in various ways; the point, however, is to *change* it'. But to this we should reply 'The point for whom?'. Sometimes Marx seems to suppose that the only good and interesting thoughts are those that are practically useful to us, but there is no reason why we should accept this stipulation. If we do not, the aspirations of philosophy and even social philosophy are quite unaffected by the truth of Marx's theory, if it is true. For we can agree that sometimes we want to change the world without agreeing that there is no point in doing anything else. We can ask, for instance, whether some social or political system is good or bad, not because we want to change it, but because we just want to *know*.

Marxists will generally argue further that such detached knowledge of good and bad is not obtainable, that there is no neutral standpoint from which to view the vices and virtues of the society in which we live. Indeed, a thoroughgoing Marxist would argue that it is only when a classless society in which there is unity rather than antagonism of interests has come about that a disinterested scrutiny of social and political institutions and arrangements is possible. But this reply is self-defeating. If *every* pre-communist society viewpoint is distorted, then so is the Marxist's own, and this includes the view that all such viewpoints are distorted. If on the other hand this belief can commend itself on impartial grounds, there must be the possiblity of assuming an objective point of view. If so, this is all that social philosophy aspires to.

This argument, I think, will be found to counter effectively almost all forms of relativism which try to circumscribe social, political, religious and moral thought on the grounds that societies and cultures cannot be viewed objectively and impartially by those who live in them. I am not concerned to rebut the general charge – a more convincing proof of the value of social philosophy will be found in actually doing it rather than in abstract arguments which purport to show that it can be done – but only to give support to my conclusion that we need not concern ourselves further with the Marxist challenge to social philosophy. Let us turn then to the second alternative.

Machiavelli

Niccolo Machiavelli was born in Florence in 1469. As was fitting for a member of a distinguished local family he came to occupy the offices of Secretary and Second Chancellor, and this involved him in diplomatic and military missions on behalf of Florence at a time of great political turbulence in what we now know as Italy. In 1512 the political masters whom Machiavelli served were defeated, and he was first excluded from political office, then imprisoned and tortured and finally, on his release, obliged to retire to the country. In an effort to put his political experience to use despite his exclusion from practical affairs, Machiavelli, who if not a great theorist was nonetheless a learned and intelligent man, wrote a little treatise entitled *The Prince*, in which he offered the new ruler of Florence the fruit of his experience as a diplomat and negotiator, in the hope, no doubt, that he might one day be reinstated in the councils of the great. The hope was quite vain, because Lorenzo the Magnificent, a member of the great Medici family and the ruler in question, paid little attention to Machiavelli or his writings. But the book nonetheless became very famous and Machiavelli, although he ended his life in relative obscurity, lent his name to a universally recognized style of politics – Machiavellianism.

The popular conception of this style of politics, and the mythology which surrounds it, have little to do with the contents of *The Prince* or the thrust of Machiavelli's arguments. There has scarcely been a tyrant – Robespierre, Mussolini, Stalin are just three of the best known – who has not been said to keep *The Prince* as bedtime reading, and in general Machiavellianism is taken to mean the blackest of the black in political skullduggery. This reputation is unfortunate chiefly because it has served to obscure the true interest in Machiavelli's writings. This interest lies in their being an early articulation of a position, which though sceptical of moralizing in social and political matters, is quite a respected one in the world at large. It is the view often known as 'political realism'.

We have seen that social philosophy is concerned with questions about the right and proper, and not merely the most successful, form of society. How should we think of society and in what ways is it right to try to organize it? Such a concern is anathema to the Marxist who thinks that these questions only have a point once certain revolutionary changes in social structure have come about. But they are equally anathema to the so-called 'realist' in politics, who thinks that in the real world those who control states and thus rule societies must be concerned not with right and wrong but with the retention of power. And such, in essence, is Machiavelli's belief.

It is wrong, however, to think of Machiavelli as the spokesman of power-hungry rulers who care nothing for justice or decency. Machiavelli believed that morality has its place, but that it cannot be given overriding importance in the conduct of social or political affairs without disastrous effect. To see why he thinks this it is necessary to dig a little below the surface of what he says and consider his conception of society and the state.

We saw earlier that there is a problem about delineating the boundaries of societies. Just where one society ends and another begins is very often, perhaps always, impossible to say. But where one *state* ends and another begins is a matter that *does* admit of an answer. This is not, in the last analysis, a legal or constitutional matter but a matter of power. Who rules effectively over which piece of territory is something which force of arms determines and law, at best, merely reflects – or so the realist thinks. Now whereas both individualists and communitarians believe a society to be the basic unit of social division, and the state merely the instrument through which social order is preserved, the Machiavellian realist thinks of the matter the other way about. For the realist it is the state which is fundamental, because a society is just that network of institutions and accompanying fellow feeling which grows up under the protection of a settled state. If so, any society survives only so long as it enjoys this protection and the first duty of those whose business is the exercise of state power is the preservation of the state through the exercise of that power. To say that this is their first duty is just to say that nothing, not even moral or religious scruple, must take priority over it. Thus, Machiavelli does not admire the ruthlessness of Cesare Borgia (one of his great heroes) for its own sake, but for the singularity of purpose which it demonstrates, something without which, in his view, society can come to nothing.

Should we take this view it may appear to follow that social theorizing of a philosophical and evaluative kind, such as this book is concerned with, will be idle from the point of view of the real business of politics. For the realistic politician is not concerned with the ideal structure of society, but with the preservation of the realm, and hence of its society, whatever structure it may have. To be concerned with the moral justification of social forms, as social philosophy is, though it may have academic interest, is a luxury which society's rulers cannot afford. It is in this sense impractical, or, in the pejorative sense, idealistic, that is, unrealistic.

Machiavelli's own arguments are neither very rigorous nor

convincing. In fact *The Prince* is a somewhat scrappy set of generalizations based on a rather special set of personal experiences. In his defence it should be said that Renaissance Italy probably was a place in which a high sense of principle was something that could be maintained only at the cost of ineffectiveness. Nevertheless, as a general view of politics and social criticism, 'realism' cannot be sustained for long. To begin with we can repeat one of the arguments raised against Marx. Where political conditions are sufficiently stable to relegate invasion or conquest to the realms of the conceivable rather than the probable, there is no reason to suppose that the necessities of power will determine every social and political question. The territorial integrity of the United Kingdom and the United States, for instance, are not seriously at risk, so that in these countries, even by the realist's account, we *can* afford the 'luxury' of critical moral thought. Some will claim that this does not follow, that the defence of these realms is, for Machiavellian reasons, of paramount importance (consider here some of the objections to moral arguments for nuclear disarmament); but even if we grant this, there is still work for social philosophy to do, assuming what is true, that defence is not the only matter on the political agenda. But the realist's overriding concern with the defence of the realm suggests a yet more fundamental objection.

The realist believes that the state must be preserved through power for its own sake. But why should we accept this? If a state is brutal and the society which it protects unjust or oppressive, what reason is there to preserve it? Its disintegration, even its invasion and conquest by another state, may be preferable. If so, realism is without foundation. Of course, realists tacitly *assume* that the state whose powers they exercise is worth preserving, so worth preserving in fact that any steps taken to this end are justified. Whether in many cases this is so may reasonably be doubted, but the main point to grasp is that their most basic appeal is to the *value* of the state and the society they wish to preserve. And any inquiry into this value, which is what social philosophy is, is therefore more basic than the principles of statecraft to which they make appeal. We may thus conclude that the Machiavellian or realist alternative to social philosophy is no alternative at all.

2

Society and the Individual

Having dealt with the objections of Marx and Machiavelli, we may return to the dispute between individualist and communitarian conceptions of society. In the last chapter I suggested that one way of trying to settle this dispute is by considering the different arguments that have have been brought by proponents of these views. This strategy, however, is not as simple as might at first appear because, in order for there to be even the hope of a result, we need to determine where the burden of proof lies. Since, unlike argument in the courts where the presumption of innocence establishes from the outset who has to prove what, there is no generally accepted principle to be appealed to here; what we need to decide is which is *initially* the more plausible view. In deciding this, however, we encounter the dispute at another level. Some people have thought it obvious that the onus is upon anyone who wants to talk of 'society' in a substantial sort of way to show that there is reason to go beyond the realm of individual human beings, a realm with which we are thoroughly familiar in everyday life. But others have thought that the concept of 'the individual' which lies behind the conception of society as an association, because it finds little place in the beliefs of most times and societies, is a European invention of the last two hundred years, the coherence and usefulness of which has yet to be demonstrated.

It might seem then that between the individualists and their opponents there is deadlock. But this can in fact be broken if we are careful to distinguish between different versions of the dispute, since different versions have different initial plausibilities.

INDIVIDUALISM VERSUS HOLISM

(b) *The ontological version*

When we ask the question 'What sort of thing is a society?' we are asking what philosophers call an *ontological* question. The word 'ontological' comes from Greek words meaning 'being' and 'reason', and applies to any theory that purports to explain what is involved in being one thing rather than another, or even what is involved in just *being* at all. An ontology of society, then, is a theory that tells us what sort of thing a society is. We saw in the last chapter that it is not at all easy to say what a society is, both because it is so hard to demarcate one society from another and because the way we generally use the word pulls us in different directions – one cultural, the other political. But independently of this, people have often been puzzled directly by what we may now call the ontological status of societies, the sorts of thing they are. Do societies exist in their own right, or is 'society' just a conveniently shorthand way of talking about the many people who comprise it?

To this question two principal answers have been given, and these answers are closely connected with the conceptions of society outlined in the last chapter, so closely connected in fact that the same terms tend to be used of them. Some people think that, ontologically speaking, there cannot be more to a society than a collection of individual human beings. What more, they think, is there for it to be? This view we may call 'ontological individualism', the belief that societies consist in nothing more than individual human beings. Other people have taken the view that societies are entities over and above the individuals who belong to them, entities which, if they do not have a physical existence like human beings, nonetheless exist independently of them since they can be referred to without any reference to any individual being made thereby. This view, which is closely connected with communitarianism, regards society as more than the sum of its members, as, that is to say, a *whole* in its own right, and for this reason is usually called 'ontological *holism*'.

The question we now want to ask is: 'Which of these views is correct?', and as I have already remarked, this means that at the outset we must decide which view is *initially* more plausible so that we may then consider the objections that may be brought against it. It will then be possible to review all the replies and counter-replies familiar to those who think about these matters.

In the case of the ontological version of the dispute it seems clear that individualism is initially a more plausible view. This is because we can construe ontological individualism in a very minimal way, namely as a doctrine that rests entirely upon two propositions, neither of which can seriously be doubted. These are that individual human beings exist, and that they may be grouped into what we call societies. As far as the strictest individualism is concerned, this is all there is to be said about the ontology of societies, and since at least this much is certainly true, the onus must be upon anyone who wishes to claim, as the holist does, that there is more to the matter than this. I shall, therefore, begin by assuming the truth of ontological individualism, and consider arguments against such a minimal conception of society, which are at the same time, of course, arguments in favour of a holist view.

Arguments for ontological holism   There are two rather obvious objections to the view that societies are nothing more than the individuals who comprise them.

First, a collection of things is not the same as a whole entity made up of those same things. Consider a human body. This is not just a *collection* of limbs, teeth, eyes and so on, but a set of these things related in certain ways. There is a great and important difference between the different members of my body being collected together in a bag, say, and their existing together in the special relations which allow them to make up a functioning human being. So too with society. When a society is overrun by famine, disease, war and so on, the people who belong to it may become refugees, wholly dependent in a parasitic way on some other society. In such circumstances it makes sense to say that, though the people remain, the society is no more, and this is because the various *relationships* which makes these people a society have broken down. It follows that society must be more than a collection of individual human beings.

Secondly, a society can continue over time even though the

collection of individuals that comprises it at any one time does not. If one were to name all members of British society on a Friday and compare it with a list of the names of members the following Sunday, the two lists would not be the same (some people would have died, others have been born), which is to say that they would be the names of different collections of people. But it is obvious that between Friday and Sunday a different *society* has not come into existence, and from this it follows that a society cannot be just a collection of people.

So, for these reasons, we must conclude that a society is more than the individuals who at any one time belong to it, something which exists in its own right. And to say this is just to agree with the thesis of ontological holism.

People are sometimes very resistant to this conclusion, however, because they think ontological holism calls into existence a strange realm of ghostly entities which somehow float about above the heads of ordinary people. But ontological holism only requires us to admit the idea of *corporate* entities, something with which all legal systems are familiar. A corporation is legally distinct from those who operate its affairs. It may buy and sell property in its own right, which is to say no more than that the company's property does not belong to any of those who buy it or sell it on the company's behalf. Further, a company may have liabilities that are not liabilities of any of its directors, and may sue or be sued in its corporate person. All these facts are thoroughly familiar and they oblige us to agree that it is wrong to think of corporate entities merely as concepts which allow us to refer in a shorthand way to the people who operate them. But this does not carry the implication that they are spirits of some sort which hover around when employees get together. Corporations have social not physical existence.

And so it is with society itself. Society is a corporate entity, because it plainly is not to be identified with some group of individual human beings. But this does not make the nature of its existence mysterious in any way, and once we see this any instinctive opposition to ontological holism should fade away. Moreover, it is easy to see that the dispute between the rival individualist and communitarian conceptions of society could not involve this ontological dispute. If the question is whether we are to regard societies as associations or communities, rather obviously this question will still remain even when we have settled the ontological status of social entities like associations and communities.

(b) The methodological version

In view of the reasons given above it is hard not to agree that societies must in some sense or other exist over and above human beings, but convinced individualists will reply that this makes no important concession to holism, because it remains the case that social entities, though not identical with sets of people, are nevertheless dependent upon the existence of human beings. That is to say, there may be no one set of individuals with which a given society can be identified, but without *some* set of individual human beings no society would exist. Moreover, this existential dependence is a one-way dependence, according to most individualists, since human beings can exist, if poorly, without there being societies. The same is true of all corporate entities.

But if this is correct, what is the connection between society and the individual? Society, we have seen, is not just individuals *en masse*, and the relation cannot be straightforwardly ontological, so we must find the connection elsewhere. Some individualists claim to have found it at the level of understanding social events. The idea is this.

Though corporations can act, they only do so through the actions of individuals. So, for instance, if General Motors invests in a new factory, it is true that the investor is the corporation rather than its executives, but it is also true that this act of investment is to be analysed and explained in terms of the actions of individuals voting at board meetings, signing pieces of paper, making phone calls, and so on. Though it is right and proper to speak of a meeting deciding upon this or that course of action, its decision is to be analysed and explained only in terms of individual decisions to vote this way or that.

This is the thesis of methodological individualism, so called because it carries the implication that the proper method of understanding and' explaining societies must reduce their behaviour to the behaviour of individual human beings. One way, though not an altogether satisfactory way, of expressing this is to say that sociological events must ultimately be explained by human psychology.

In illustration of this thesis consider the case of an army. An army cannot be identified with its personnel for the sorts of reasons already rehearsed. Its existence as an army is not the existence of a mere collection of human beings. Nevertheless, in understanding and explaining the behaviour of the army – its tactics, strategy, victories and defeat – there is nothing further to be explained once we have explained the decisions of all the relevant human beings. And it is this apparent truth that methodological individualism points to.

Arguments for methodological holism   But the argument cannot end here. The clear thinking holist has at least two replies to make to this methodological version of individualism.

First, to think of society as a mere *grouping* of human beings is to think of those human beings as anterior to it, that is, existing as living human beings *before* being grouped together. This is the view that the belief in a one-way existential dependence expresses, in fact. But is it so obvious that people can exist without societies? The fact is that people are more than animals, and what makes up the extra is their self-understanding, the understanding in terms of which their plans and aspirations are formed. But this understanding is itself *social*. People think of themselves and their lives, including those career plans which are most properly called 'self-chosen', in irreducibly social concepts. For example, a life as self-concerned as one devoted to making money and owning property is necessarily conceived in terms of 'buying', 'selling', 'banking', 'interest', all of which are social not individualistic concepts. In fact, deprived of social relations, it is doubtful if the individual could have a recognizably human life at all.

The second argument for methodological holism is suggested by Marx's famous dictum (made, perhaps, with this dispute in mind), 'Men make their own history, but they do not make it just as they choose'. Methodological individualism supposes that any adequate explanation of social events will ultimately have to appeal to the actions and motivations of individuals and that this appeal will be wholly adequate. But this ignores the important fact that many large-scale social events are plainly determined in part by factors beyond the control of individuals.

This is not the same as saying that many social events are not under the control of any one individual. The famous eighteenth-century Scottish economist Adam Smith drew attention to what are now called (using an expression of his) 'invisible hand' explanations. The clearest example of this sort of thing is the price of any good in a free market. In a free market no one buyer or seller can fix the price. But there is no extra-human agency at work. It is the combined transactions of all buyers and sellers which determine it. This is a good example for methodological individualism because in explaining the price of some good, though we acknowledge that no human agency fixes it, we need nevertheless appeal to nothing more than human agency in general. It is explanations of this sort with which economics very often concerns itself.

Invisible hand explanations work well in conditions approximating to a free market, which should be understood as a world of trading which is governed by no antecedently established institutions. Such markets are rare, and where they exist they are desirable, or thought to be so, because they allow the free transactions of a great many individuals to result in the satisfaction of each and the greatest benefit of all. But where free market conditions do not obtain, the interactions of the many can result in the disbenefit of all. For example, it may be to the advantage of everyone that expensive measures are taken to control the emission of sulphur from electricity plants because of the highly damaging acid rain that these emissions cause. But it is plainly to the disadvantage of any one supplier to install this expensive equipment unless nearly everyone else does, because in such circumstances the supplier who did so would have all the costs of environmental controls and none of the benefits. But this applies to everyone and consequently, so long as each believes that too few people will take similar measures to secure this commonly advantageous end, each will act in a way that results overall in a consequence that nobody wants. In such circumstances people are making their own history, but not as they choose.

This is an instance of what is known as a co-ordination problem. Such problems raise deep and difficult questions in moral theory, but their relevance here is that they provide counter-instances to methodological individualism because they show that appeal to the motives and actions of individuals may not be enough to explain social phenomena. In the example just given, what explains the outcome is not only the desires and wishes of the human agents involved, but the absence of social or political institutions that would allow the co-ordination of a common policy. That there is no such institution is not a fact about human nature or about the psychology of individuals, but a *social* fact, a fact about the society in which the human agents in question take their decisions. This means that methodological individualism is false; the explanation of social events and conditions cannot always be given by reference to the actions and purposes of individuals.

(c) The political version

We have seen, I think, that there is no reason to insist upon the ontological or the methodological priority of individual human beings over societies. Societies exist over and above the individuals who comprise them, and social concepts and facts are as much involved in the explanation of the behaviour of the individual as individual motivation is involved in the explanation of social phenomena. We might suppose, therefore, that individualism has been thoroughly routed in this dispute. But if we look more carefully at the motivations of those who have argued against holism we will see that nothing of real importance has been lost.

Holism has been associated with totalitarianism. At the time of the First World War a celebrated liberal theorist called Hobhouse argued that holism, which he called *The Metaphysical Theory of the State* (the title of one of his best known books) was responsible for the attitudes and actions of imperial aggrandizement, and in a very famous book entitled *The Poverty of Historicism* (1957) Sir Karl Popper argued, against Marxists, that the persecutions in communist countries were a result of subscription to the holist conception of society. Popper says holism's belief that society is more than the individuals who comprise it gives a licence to those who wish to curtail the rights and freedoms of the individual in the name of 'Society's' greater good. Holism thus becomes the justificatory theory of tyranny.

But this argument cannot be correct. We can believe that animals exist independently of those who breed them, without having any view on the relative moral importance of breeder and stock, and similarly we can hold that societies exist independently of human beings without thereby committing ourselves to beliefs about one being more important than the other. We can also hold that all that happens and is important to human beings is not to be explained entirely in terms of individual motivations and actions, and hold, nevertheless, that its *importance* is to be explained by appeal to the desires and interests of individuals.

This way of putting the matter opens up the possibility of another sort of individualism, which we may call 'political individualism' because it is a *political* rather than an ontological or a methodological doctrine. It is the view that social policies and state actions are to be judged good or bad only in so far as they serve the desires and purposes of individual members of society. No doubt a great deal needs to be said about such a principle by way of clarification and amplification, but even as it stands it clearly expresses a belief in the individual as the touchstone, not of social existence or social explanation, but of social *value*.

We should notice too that political individualism need not be thought to rely in some sense upon an ideal which pre-exists social life. Locke's conception of political society as an association of individuals giving up a 'state of nature' was conceived in historical terms, and has often been criticized on the grounds that there is no historical evidence for thinking that there ever was such a state of nature, or a coming together out of it. But we can agree that this is so, and still subscribe to political individualism as an emergent rather than an antecedent ideal, believing the state of perfect liberty, which Locke ascribes to primitive men, to be something towards which society and the state should aim, rather than something from which they have arisen. And if we do think of it in this way, we can freely admit that social forms and forces have their part to play in explaining how it might come about. But we must first ask whether there is good reason to accept it.

If we define political individualism as the belief that state action and social policy must be judged good or bad as they affect the interests and purposes of the individual, we may define its opposite, political holism, as the view that the actions and interests of the individual must be subservient to the good of society as this is represented in the state. Such a view, or something like it, is to be found most obviously in the writings of Fascists, but it has a currency and a plausibility that this observation obscures. It is not only Fascists who have held this belief but a wide range of conservatives, socialists and nationalists as well. Political holism, in fact, will have attractions for all those who are inclined to think of society as a community, one of the conceptions of society set out in the last chapter. For it is not difficult to find in ourselves attachments to the traditions and values with which the society to which we belong is peculiarly associated, and to see a value in the maintenance and perpetuation of those values, irrespective of their immediate bearing upon the lives of individuals. To subscribe to political holism, then, is not to be some species of unthinking fanatic. There are, as we shall see, good, though not conclusive, arguments to be advanced in its favour.

Arguments for political holism   First, we have seen that a society is more than a collection of individuals and extends over time. From this it follows that future and past individuals have a legitimate interest in present social policy and that, accordingly, the test of good and bad in social policy cannot be assessed entirely in terms of the individuals who comprise the society when that social policy is being decided upon.

That future members of society have interests in present policy is difficult to deny. Since what we do now will affect the health and happiness of our children and their children, and since the health and happiness of people matters, future generations matter. Just how the interests of future generations are to be evaluated in the political calculation is not so easy to say, but the main difficulty with the argument we are considering will probably be thought to lie with the claim that *past* members have legitimate interests in present policy also.

But is this so hard to understand? We are all familiar with the device by which the dead effect present decisions, namely legal wills, and, even if we do not think the duty to honour the wishes of the dead paramount, it is difficult to deny that, other things being equal, *something* is owed to their desires, since these desires do not, in the fullest sense, die with them.

Even if we agree with this view of the dead and the yet to be born, however, it provides no support for political holism, which is the view, after all, that the interests of the individual, past, present or future, are subservient to those of society as a whole. To show that past and future individuals have interests in the present is not to show anything about the relative importance of those interests compared to the interests of society, if such there be. Edmund Burke and other conservative thinkers have often been anxious to stress the unity of society over time, as an antidote to obsessive concern with the present, but however salutary this lesson may be, it goes no distance towards establishing the greater value of society.

A second argument for political holism runs as follows. There are *general* interests, *social* benefits and *public* goods. These cannot be identified with the interests of individuals. Consequently the protection and promotion of these interests, which must be the responsibility of the state, is not the same as the protection and promotion of the interests of individuals, from which it follows that the state has obligations other than those to individuals.

To appreciate the force of this argument we need to look a little more closely at the idea of a public good, a concept which will be employed at later stages in any case. Some goods (a 'good' being a general term used to cover any object or opportunity we find valuable) are called private because their consumption by one person prevents their consumption by anyone else. Food is obviously a private good, for you cannot eat the apple I have just eaten. So are clothes (only one of us can wear a particular sweater at any one time) as are very many other goods. But some goods are not like this. The most obvious cases are publicly provided goods, for instance streetlighting. If the street is lit for me, it is lit for you also, and the benefit I derive from it is not diminished in any way by your deriving benefit from it also. Defence provides another example. If a country is defended against foreign attack, additional towns and citizens can enjoy the resultant security without detracting from the security enjoyed by existing towns and citizens.

Public goods, then, may be defined as goods whose benefits cannot be confined to or exclusively associated with any one set of named individuals. Such goods are very important in the discussion of a great many issues in social philosophy because a question arises whether those people who benefit from public goods to the cost of which they contribute nothing (generally called 'free-riders') can justifiably be forced (through taxation) to make a contribution, since they do not benefit at anyone else's expense. At this point in our argument, however, the importance public goods have (or might be thought to have) for the discussion of political individualism is this. The claim that the state can only justifiably defend the lives, freedom and property of individuals can now be rejected, it appears, on the grounds that there are these public goods, goods which the state plainly ought to promote and defend but which are not the property of individuals.

Given the evident fact that there are public goods, this counter-claim can hardly be denied. But political individualism is not so easily defeated. Though no one can deny the public character of such goods, it seems pretty plain that our considering them goods or benefits at all relies upon our being individualists at least to the extent that we take the satisfaction of human desires to be the touchstone of social value. If streetlighting, defence, sewage systems and the like did not serve the sorts of ends that individuals value (such as avoiding injury, conflict, homelessness and disease), what reason would there be to call them public *goods*? The obvious implication of this rhetorical question is that at the heart of social assessment we must indeed place the interests of the individual.

Someone might reply that public services of the sort we have been considering do not provide the right kind of example for the claim that the state has purposes and duties other than those that arise from the purposes of individual human beings. Rather we should consider the prestige projects that can only be undertaken by communities as a whole. Consider, for instance, space exploration. We quite naturally describe this, not as a race between the individual scientists and astronauts involved, but as a race between the United States and the Soviet Union (and some others), and equally naturally we consider any achievement, like being first on the moon, as a *national* achievement. Similarly, in the past great victories on the battlefield have been regarded as the achievements of peoples or nations, as are sporting successes today, and the point to be drawn from such ways of thinking and speaking is that a society may have goals and accomplishments of its own, over and above the accomplishments of the individuals belonging to it.

But even faced with these phenomena the political individualist need not concede defeat. However grand and extensive national or communal projects may be, it remains the fact that we can only lend sense to the claim that the state should promote and protect them if we can show that they are the sorts of project in which individuals can take satisfaction. If we could imagine a project of staggering difficulty, say digging an enormous crater in some remote part of the world, which could generate no interest or satisfaction on the part of individuals, it is well-nigh impossible to see any grounds upon which any state might reasonably be urged to undertake it. This is because in the consideration of political projects the individual is in an important sense ineliminable. Though a society may have an existence and a unity of its own, it has neither hands nor feet. Individual human agents must decide upon and be motivated to realize any state or public action. Consequently it is to those values which can actually motivate individuals that appeal must ultimately be made.

This reply, it might be said, begs the question, for it supposes that the only projects in which individuals may interest themselves are the projects *of* individuals, and from this a third argument for political holism may be drawn. It rests upon a direct rejection of what it perceives to be a false ideal. Political individualism, in the view of its critics, appears to rely upon an ideal of the individual which is both morally objectionable and psychologically unrealistic, an ideal which has come to be known as that of the 'possessive individual'. It thus supposes, not that the state should serve the purposes of the individuals, but that it should serve the purposes of a certain *sort* of individual, namely the ruggedly independent type which is commonly thought to have founded the American colonies and peopled their expansion, especially into the mid-west. But if this is so, political individualism is really a doctrine that appeals to the selfish, those who can find importance only in those things that are theirs. If such individuals exist there is, the holist believes, no reason to structure society or the state exclusively to their liking. Indeed there is reason *not* to do so, because in the main human beings are not self-sufficient and fiercely independent, but desire and require a sense of belonging to something other and larger than themselves, a desire that is evidenced by the feelings and enthusiasm that accompany international sport. If this is so, it is the holist state, a state concerning itelf with ends and projects that are *not* exclusively geared to the purposes of individuals, which is more likely to be acceptable to the general run of citizens and hence enjoy a greater political stability.

This argument for holism is rather harder to attack than the first two because it makes appeal to an undoubted and important fact – people *do* have patriotic and nationalistic feelings – and it seems reasonable to think that the state may legitimately reflect these. Moreover, these feelings and their organization in the state can produce what appear to be morally more admirable attitudes. Readiness to take up arms in the defence of one's country, and perhaps a willingness to die for it, look like more fitting subjects for epic poems and remembrance day services than the grudging calculations of the individual who sees that his or her purposes will best be served if, reluctantly, he or she agrees to go to war.

But even this charge against individualism will be found upon examination to be ineffective and less than just, since it rests upon a travesty of the individualist ideal. Political individualism as we have been considering it, does not rely upon the belief that every justification of state and social policy must come down in the end to an appeal to the selfishness or self-centredness of individuals. It supposes only that all justifications must end in the *interests* of individuals, and these may in fact be highly unselfish, because the existence and happiness of others are often amongst the things that are in one's interest.

So, for instance, individualists can easily account for the obligation to defend one's country. What they insist upon is that the desirability of defending any country must be explained ultimately by its being a defence of the lives, liberty and happiness of individual human beings; that there is no value to the defence of one's country, just because it is a *country*.

Nor need political individualists admire the rugged self-sufficient colonialist, or deny that human beings have communal feelings. What they deny is that the focus of these communal feelings must be society, or that they are rightly embodied in the *state*. This is not the same as asserting that they need no focus or are improperly embodied anywhere. The difference is perhaps most easily illustrated by reference to the traditional liberal view of religion and politics. Individualists need not deny the value of church membership. They may even actively encourage people to join precisely because churches provide institutional expression of and reinforcement for the communal feelings which are such an important part of most people's lives. Where they draw the line is at making membership of any church *compulsory* on these grounds, because they see no justification for obliging one person to endorse the religious belief or feeling of another. The existence of rugged individualists, if there are such people, is relevant just in so far as it reminds us that such people would have the same difficulty in belonging to a holist society whose institutions were intended to express national or patriotic feeling, that a hard-bitten atheist would have in being obliged to go to church. The crucial aspect of the question is not the nature of human beings but the coercive character of society and the state, the fact that we cannot but belong to one and be subject to the other. We need special reasons for compelling human beings to behave in one way rather than another. Individualists can be firm believers in the value and importance of churches, clubs and societies. Where they differ from the holist is in their belief that all such associations must be *voluntary*.

Holism and elitism

We have been considering arguments in favour of political holism and found them to be unsatisfactory. There seems no good reason to deny that social policies and state actions are to be judged good or bad according to their effect upon the interests and purposes of individuals. But to concede this is not to have secured the ideals normally thought to be those of political individualism, for much that is associated with political holism is in fact compatible with this concession.

We can take as an example compulsory taxation, that is, the coercive collection of a large part of the earnings of individuals, and its subsequent expenditure on some prestige project like space exploration. On the surface, at any rate, a holist can believe (where an individualist cannot) that this can be justified on the grounds that it will redound to the glory of the state, even if it cannot be expected to make any significant contribution to the health, prosperity or defence of individual citizens, past, present or future. But if we look a little more closely at any such project we will see that the elimination of individual interest is really impossible. What is the value of glory, what could it possibly be, if there really were not one individual who relished it or took satisfaction in it? Why would anyone propose or support such a project if it had no connection with anything they could perceive to be in their interest? The truth is that even Fascists, the most obvious political holists of the modern period, did not think the glory of the state could be assessed or promoted independently of the evaluations of individuals. They thought, rather, that while the horizons, and hence purposes, of most individuals were corrupted by liberalism, there were certain favoured people who were able to discern and appreciate the value of the state as such, and it was by the light of the chosen purposes of these individuals, the Leaders, that accordingly they proposed to be guided. Furthermore, the actions of those Leaders were commendable precisely because they would lead to the greater good of less enlightened members of the state.

What this implied, in fact, was not that the purposes of individuals could be dispensed with, but only that those of *some*, perhaps most, individuals could be ignored, and the judgements of others could be taken as altogether superior. Thus political holism (usually called statism or corporatism in its Fascist versions because of its belief in a corporate state in which each individual has and knows his or her station and its duties) may be understood as a conception of society and the state which elevates the beliefs and preferences of some individuals over others, rather than a conception which eliminates the idea of justification by individual preference altogether.

The point may be illustrated from Plato's *Republic*, referred to briefly in the first chapter. Plato thought that the business of the state was to realize 'The Good' in a hierarchically ordered society, but he also thought that the point of so doing lay in the fact that such a society would be in the best interests of its individual members. Neither did he imagine that good government removed the need for individual reflection and purpose. Far from it. Crucial to his social theory was the belief that society could never be properly organized until certain carefully selected individuals – the philosopher-kings – came to rule, and these rulers were to be understood as those who exclusively knew and were inspired by the Good. On such a conception, plainly, the projects of the state must be justified by appeal to the interests of individuals, but *views about* those interests are to be sought and valued only from those individuals equipped to offer an informed opinion.

If this analysis is correct, we should conclude that in addition to the differences between political holism and political individualism we have discussed so far, there is a further and highly important difference between those who believe in a ruling hierarchy and those who believe in the fundamental equality of members of society. Since these alternatives make up a large part of the difference between individualists and their critics, this means that the definition of individualism which was offered earlier has to be amplified to include belief in not merely the overriding importance of individuals but also their fundamental *equality*.

But it is equality of a special sort, and we must be careful in our formulations of it. For the bald claim that human beings are equal is far from self-evident. In fact it is false. We know very well that in most intellectual matters, in matters of skill and dexterity, and in the somewhat broader virtues of thoughtfulness and common sense, human beings are *not* equal. Some are narrow-minded, shortsighted, prejudiced or just not very intelligent compared to others in the management of their businesses, marriages, families and professions. Why then should we suppose that they are equal when it comes to judging which things are right and good for society at large? The creed of most of us in most activities is 'Let the best person win' whether it be a contest or a contract. Should we not likewise subscribe to the principle 'Let the best person rule'? Why should the political purposes of some not be preferred to those of others if they are more intelligent or humane?

We might call the view that the most suited should govern 'elitism', and though it is highly unfashionable as a doctrine, its central contentions are indisputable. For there can be no denying that there are good rulers and bad, and the most elemental principle of rational conduct requires us to prefer the better to the worse. Such simple truths are unpalatable because, no doubt, they seem to attack all that is central to democracy. But the fact, if it is one, that elitism is incompatible with democracy cannot alter the truth of the two propositions which lie at its heart – people are *not* all equally capable of decision-making, and a rationally defensible constitution must prefer better to worse.

There is, however, an aspect of the matter that elitism, at least in its practical expression, tends to ignore. Some decisions *ought* to be left to those less able to make them, just because, whatever their ability, they alone have the *right* to make them. For example, if you have been given a sum of money as a present, you alone have the right to decide how it should be spent. It may well be that your taste and your common sense are demonstrably inferior to mine, so much so that if the decision were left to me a better purchase would undoubtedly be made, but for all that the decision *ought* to be left with you (though of course this includes the possibility that you will decide in accordance with my advice). To see why it ought to, and the bearing of this upon political individualism and the equality of human beings in society, we need to turn to the topics of rights and autonomy.

RIGHTS AND AUTONOMY

As human beings we are much concerned with our welfare and the welfare of others. This is to say that our health, happiness and prosperity are amongst the major concerns that structure the existence of almost every human being. But though welfare is very important it is not overridingly important. There is at least one other thing that we value as much and this is our freedom or autonomy. Autonomy is a better word than freedom here because we are not immediately concerned with a political notion, like civil liberty, but with a moral ideal – self-determination – which expresses the value we attach to doing things for ourselves, however much well or badly we do them and however better others might do them for us.

The value of self-determination is most easily perceived in the desire we all share to move from childhood to adulthood, which just is the move from having things decided for us to deciding them for ourselves. It is important to notice that we do not value self-determination or autonomy because its possession makes us happy (though to be deprived of it would indeed make most people unhappy), but for its own sake. Tiny children who are almost completely lacking in autonomy may be as healthy and happy as anyone could ever hope to be; and the idea of a 'happy slave', someone who is thoroughly content to have all decisions taken for him or her and flourishes under such a regime, is not a contradiction in terms. We value autonomy – self-direction – for its own sake.

The relevance of the value of autonomy to the dispute between political individualism and political holism is this. While it may be true that others would be better at taking certain decisions than I would, and that, in general, whoever is best at decision-making should be given the responsibility for it, it does not follow that the decision should not remain with me. This is because there are some decisions which I have a *right* to make, and which no one, however superior in skill or intelligence, has a right to take for me without my agreement. And with that right goes the possibility of taking the wrong decision, which is to say (paradoxical though it may sound) that sometimes it is right to let the wrong decision be taken.

Now if *political* decisions were of this kind, it would follow that the elitist beliefs of the holist could be accepted without any consequent commitment to a corporate state in which each person is allocated a place according to his or her intelligence and abilities. And in this way the *relevant* equality of human beings would be preserved, namely the equal right of all to take decisions for themselves, without any need to deny evident inequalities of intelligence, benevolence and so on.

But are political decisions of this sort? To put the matter simply, are voters concerned with what is best for them in the polls? If we now reintroduce the distinction between public and private goods the answer would appear to be plainly 'no'. Some actual political decisions do relate to the individual's welfare exclusively, but others plainly relate to a more general interest, the interest of all and its furtherance through the promotion and protection of public goods. But public goods, though they are important to the welfare of individuals, are not the concern of any particular set of individuals. Consequently the right to take decisions regarding them cannot be uniquely associated with any particular set of people.

If we bear in mind the distinction between public and private goods and assume without further argument that autonomy is an important human value, we are now in a position to state the thesis of political individualism in an expanded form, one which takes account of the preceding arguments. The original version was this: social policies and state actions must be judged good or bad in so far as they serve the interests of individuals. But Platonic dictators could promote the interests of their citizens, and might do so better than the citizens would do left to themselves, and so we need the following alteration: social policies and state actions must be judged good or bad only in so far as they serve the *self-chosen purposes* of individuals.

But to this revised form of political individualism the holist's objection is clear. There are public decisions to be taken that do not directly concern the welfare of individuals, but rather the combined interests of all, where 'all' here must be taken to include potential as well as actual citizens. It is this objection we now need to address.

THE INDIVIDUAL AND THE STATE

We have seen that a belief in the value of autonomy requires us to accord to individuals the right to make certain decisions for themselves, regardless of how well or badly they may decide them. If so, the crucial question becomes: which decisions? If decisions concerning social policy are included, the right of individuals to decide for themselves plainly has important and widespread implications. If, on the other hand, it is only over a limited range of 'personal' matters that individuals have an incontrovertible right to autonomy, the nature and content of public decision-making will be largely unaffected by this right. To settle this matter we need to look a little more closely at what autonomy means.

Individuals have interests. In philosophy this means something very general, namely that they have families, careers, hobbies, skills, investments, clubs, houses and so on about which they care, and that it is the pursuit and protection of these which makes life worth living. Clearly, there are many assets and actions which will help or hinder these interests, so that decisions obviously need to be made about what should be done *in* the interests of any one individual. The belief in autonomy is a belief that the individual in whose interest some action is to be taken is the person who has the right to say whether or not it should be done. In other words the individual has a right to decide for him or herself how his or her interest should be promoted. But, as we observed in the last section, the belief in such a right carries the implication both that individuals must be left to make the wrong decisions, and that they must take responsibility for their own decisions, right or wrong. The contrary belief, that the interests of individuals should, at least within limits, be protected from the foolish decision-making of the individuals themselves, is called 'paternalism'. A paternalist society is one in which the crucial test is whether social policies and the actions of the state will promote the well-being of its members, regardless of whether it is right for the *state* to be taking such decisions. An individualist society, on the other hand, is one in which the well-being of individuals takes second place to their freedom to decide things for themselves.

Of course this does not imply that individuals must do everything for themselves. I can ask, pay or elect someone to represent my interest and delegate many of the decisions to my representative. We do this all the time with lawyers, doctors, stockbrokers, architects and so on. But a representative who takes certain decisions for me takes them on my behalf, not in my place, and I retain both the final authority and the final responsibility for those decisions.

Now many social policy decisions are taken in the interests of those to whom they apply. If we believe that such decisions belong by right to those whom they affect, we will have to satisfy ourselves that those who have the right to make them are indeed making them, either directly or through representatives. This is the principle which lies behind the conception of society as an association of individuals who combine together for mutual benefit, set out in the last chapter. According to this conception, the state, though it has coercive powers, relies for its legitimacy on the consent of the governed of whom it is the representative. This way of thinking has the following implications. First, individuals have at least one right, the right to pursue their own interests as they think best (self-determination), which puts an absolute moral constraint on the kinds of social policy and state action which can be justified. From this it follows, secondly, that *un*limited states cannot be justified, since there are some things which the state cannot do to or for the individual.

The view that *all* political decisions and state actions are taken on behalf of the individual is the most extreme form of political individualism. If we add to this the belief that individuals could actually do for themselves what governments generally do on their behalf, we may conclude that societies can do without states, a view that may be called 'anarchist'. But many individualists deny this second contention and believe there to be certain important functions that only a state can fulfil. They also believe, however, that the state should have only those functions which the state really must have, and that these are in fact rather limited. Such people are often called 'libertarians'. A third category of individualist believes that the state may justifiably undertake a great many tasks on behalf of the individual if this works to the good of all, but that there are some aspects of human life so fundamental that they must always be left to individuals themselves. These are usually thought to be freedom in the pursuit of religion, morality and knowledge. This third sort of individualism we may call 'liberal'.

It must be noted immediately, however, that the employment

of these labels does not reflect uniform use. Nor is it meant to establish a recommended use. Labels, and especially political labels, tend to be applied somewhat randomly and over time can come to mean all things to all men. The three terms employed here – 'anarchist', 'libertarian' and 'liberal' – have been applied both in the theory and practice of politics to views somewhat different from those outlined here. For instance, there are anarchists who are not individualists at all. They believe strongly in the values of community, but hold that the best communities will be stateless. In the United States, people who believe that the activities of the state should be severely limited are usually called 'conservatives', and it is those who believe in limiting the liberties of the individual in trade, education and defence who are, partly for that reason, called 'liberals'. What this shows is that it is impossible to *fix* political or social labels. But this does not mean that they cannot usefully be used to some purpose, and the purpose here is to mark three positions on a spectrum of opinion about the degree to which the state and society should be limited in their involvement in the life of the individual: the 'anarchist' holds that they should have no role at all, the 'libertarian' that they should have a very minimal role, and the 'liberal' that their role should be limited in some ways.

We are now in a position to answer in outline one of the most important questions in social philosophy and policy, namely: what is a free society? The individualist's answer is: any society in which individuals are as free as possible to pursue their own interests as they think best. Just how far this *is* possible is a matter on which the different varieties of individualism I have just outlined disagree and we will pursue something of this disagreement in the context of specific social issues. But first we should turn to a contrasting view.

We saw in chapter 1 that the individualist conception of society is to be contrasted with a communitarian one. So too, and in a connected way, is the emphasis on autonomy to be contrasted with a different virtue, a distinctively social one. Whereas a free society, as we have just described it, is one in which a value attaching to individual human beings – autonomy – is realized to the greatest degree, a just society is one in which a *social* value – social justice – is realized. At least, this is one way of looking at justice in society, and it is a way that is characteristic of many communitarian views of society. Moreover, to raise the question of justice here is to bring into play the second of the two sorts of argument I advocated as a means of investigating the dispute between individualism and communitarianism – namely an examination of the social implications of each.

It has long been a claim of the critics of individualism that an individualistic society cannot be a just one, and that the choice between individualism and communitarianism is at least in part a choice between freedom and justice. If this is true, the fact that a wholly free society would be radically unjust would give us a reason to reject the individualist conception of society as an association. To discover whether or not it *is* true, we need to look more closely at the conception of social justice. But before that it seems sensible to summarize the argument so far.

SUMMARY

In chapter 1 I outlined two competing conceptions of society. According to the first of these, which we have called 'individualism', we should think of society as an association of self-determining individuals, each with his or her own purposes which social living facilitates. If we do think in this way, we will readily conclude that the state which conducts the general affairs of such a society will be a limited one, one, that is to say, for which certain actions are out of bounds. This is because there are some decisions about some matters which individuals must be left to decide for themselves because they have a right to decide them for themselves. Just where the limits of the individualist state lie is a matter for further investigation, but wherever we draw the line, there will still be a contrast with the sort of state appropriate to society conceived of as a community. A community has an integrity and a value over and above that which attaches to the individuals who belong to it, and accordingly, if we take this view, the state will be thought of as the custodian of the interests of the community and not merely the protector of the interests of individuals within it.

Which conception of society ought we to adopt? The answer to this question depends on the cogency of the arguments that may be advanced in favour of and against each of them, and the social policy implications which each entails. If we turn first to the arguments we find that there are a number of different strands to the dispute between individualism and its critics, which we can distinguish as the ontological, methodological and political versions. Beginning with a presumption in favour of ontological individualism, on the grounds that it is the more plausible view initially, we were led to the conclusion that it is nevertheless false, and that we have no reason to accept methodological individualism either. But the elimination of both these versions still leaves *political* individualism intact, and the arguments which holists have traditionally brought against it seem to be unsuccessful.

There is, however, a second strategy. We can reject an individualist conception of society on the grounds that it has unacceptable implications of a moral kind, which are revealed when we look in more detail at the sort of society it favours. In employing this sort of argument, of course, we must be careful to balance deeply held convictions about what is acceptable and what is unacceptable, with what reasoned argument tells us we should accept. As we shall see, in fact, this sort of balancing is made possible by the process of clarification itself, for in considering precisely what the implications are, we also see precisely how objectionable (or unobjectionable) they are.

It is to an argument of this sort that we now turn. Individualistic conceptions of society, it is often said, give pride of place to freedom at the expense of justice. An individualistically conceived society is inevitably an unjust one. To see what force there is in this charge we must obviously examine the concept of social justice. This is the subject of the next chapter.

3

Social Justice

In social philosophy we want to know chiefly what society *is*. Another way of saying this is that we want to know which conception of society we ought to employ. But to have an answer to this question will not provide solutions to all the questions and problems social philosophy encounters, especially those concerned with social policy. To answer many of these we also want to know in more detail what sort of society we ought to commend.

On this score, I have suggested, we must take some account of what sorts of social arrangement are generally regarded as morally acceptable. This is not to say that we must be dictated to by conventional wisdom: rather that at some point or other we must appeal to recognized and accepted social *values*.

Of course, many important disagreements in social philosophy seem to turn on disagreements over values, so that the strategy of appealing to accepted social values might be thought doomed from the outset. But there are at least four social values over which there is almost no disagreement, namely peace, prosperity, freedom and justice. Pretty well everyone wants to live in a peaceful and prosperous society, where they are free and where justice prevails, and consequently it is to these values that we may make appeal.

This is not to say that such values are incontestable, or have never been contested. Prosperity as an aspiration for the individual has been questioned by mystics and ascetics, like Francis of Assisi, though it has probably never been seriously disputed as a virtue of *societies*. On the other hand, the peace for which most of us hope nowadays would not have commended itself to many in the ancient world. Even today in certain parts of the world, fighting is regarded as a highly honourable human activity, a belief shared perhaps by some on the football terraces

of the West. But no modern politician would actually campaign
in the cause of war for its own sake, and no contemporary social
theory is built around the rejection of peace.

   With freedom and justice the position is a little different. No
one openly denies the value of these. No one campaigns for an
unfree or an unjust society. Disagreement arises rather over
their interpretation and over the relative importance of each.
Precisely what counts as a free society and precisely what social
justice is are hotly contested questions. Furthermore, many
theorists (and others) have claimed that freedom and justice are
in competition, so that we must decide which is to have priority
over the other. Generally speaking, individualists stress the
importance of individual liberty and communitarians stress the
importance of social justice. What we need to do, therefore, is
address these questions.

DISTRIBUTIVE AND RETRIBUTIVE JUSTICE

We have defined the free society as one in which individuals are
as free as possible to decide for themselves on those matters that
affect their interests. There is more that needs to be said about
this, and we will have to consider the application of this idea of
a free society further later on. First, though, in order to see
whether and how far it conflicts with social justice we must
consider what social justice is.

   We should begin by drawing a distinction very familiar to
social and political philosophers, the distinction between
retributive and distributive justice. Retributive justice is the sort
of justice that is invoked in the criminal law. Its fundamental
maxim is that all and only those who break the law should be
punished, and this shows from the start that retributive justice is
concerned with crime and punishment. But not all matters of
justice are matters of crime and punishment. In particular, the
distribution of burdens and benefits can be just or unjust,
though no question of punishment arises. There is a celebrated
story in the New Testament about an employer who took on
workers for his vineyard at different points over the day. Some
started early in the morning and some did not begin till almost
evening. With each group the employer agreed, unknown to

the rest, on the same payment. When at the end of the day everyone was paid the same amount of money, despite the fact that some had done much more work than others, those who had started early complained. And their complaint was not that some crime had been committed by the other workers and gone unpunished, but that the distribution of rewards was unjust.

What made it unjust, if it was? In the story, the vineyard owner rejects the complaints of the workers. They all, he says, freely made agreements with him, and it was in accordance with those agreements that payment was made, payment consisting, after all, in money which was his to do with as he liked. It is the possibility and plausibility of this reply which shows how freedom and justice might be thought to conflict, for the free interaction of employer and labourers has led, it appears, to an unjust result.

But is it really unjust? The purpose of this chapter is to examine what distributive justice in a society is, and indeed whether there really is such a thing, and in what ways if any it conflicts with the freedom of the individual. It is best, though, to begin by clearing away some common confusions and saying what social justice is *not*.

What social justice is not

The satisfaction of basic needs When people look at the distribution of wealth in society they are often most concerned about hardship and suffering. That is to say, what moves them to think about the subject at all is the actual condition of the poor rather than their relative poverty. It is when we see shanty town children and the like that our belief in the need for 'society' to do something is usually kindled. Sometimes it is supposed that such conditions would not prevail in a just society, which is the same as saying that to suffer hardship and poverty is itself to suffer injustice.

This identification of social justice with the meeting of needs is common but it is plainly wrong, because it confuses justice with prosperity, albeit prosperity on a low level, and the well-being of individuals with a just social order. But because there is no reason to believe that the world owes anyone a living, we cannot conclude from the mere fact that someone is not actually making a living that an obligation is not being met or an injustice being done. Harvests and businesses fail through no one's fault sometimes, and hence through no injustice, and a solitary islander who starves to death, though to be pitied, has not been done an injustice. Conversely, sometimes basic needs fail to be met through the fault of the person whose needs they are, and once again this shows that the fact that basic needs are not being met cannot warrant the inference that there is injustice. For example, if a newspaper were to report the case of an individual whose life is threatened because some vital organ is not functioning properly, and that, though there are plenty of hospitals where an operation could be performed to remedy this, no hospital would perform it without payment of a fee far higher than anything the individual in question could afford, many people would take this to be definitive of a case of social injustice. But if it turns out that the person concerned needs a liver transplant as a result of a lifetime's excess drinking, and that he cannot afford the operation only because he has twice cashed in his state-provided insurance policy to spend on footling extras, it will be evident that the truth of the first report is not a sufficient warrant for thinking that there is social injustice here.

The recognition of merit   One response to this sort of example is to try to build in the importance of *merit*. Social justice requires us not to meet the needs of the poor and destitute but the innocent or deserving poor and destitute. But upon reflection this amendment does not seem to give us a very satisfactory conception of justice either. We can too easily think of examples in which those who *deserve* certain benefits (or punishments) are nevertheless not *entitled* to them. So, for instance, someone who has trained hard and has great talent may deserve to win the race and take the prize, but if, by an unlucky accident, she should stumble on the home straight and another, less talented or hardworking athlete should take the lead and cross the line, though the first may deserve the prize, the second is entitled to it and it would plainly be an injustice to deny her it.

If this analysis is correct we must conclude that neither the satisfaction of needs, even of a very basic kind, nor the recognition of desert can be what social justice is about. To put the matter at its plainest, we may need things, and even deserve them, while having no right to them. Conversely, we may have a right to things which we neither need nor deserve.

It might be supposed that what is missing from the analysis is any sort of comparison between different groups in society. A question of social justice surely arises not simply where there is suffering and hardship, but where there is suffering and hardship *alongside* wealth and affluence. What people object to in shanty towns is not merely the misery and degradation that is to be found in them, but their proximity, very often, to sumptuous boulevards and leafy suburbs. It is the comparison of the two, not the shanty town on its own, that gives rise to a sense of injustice.

Equality   The idea that questions of social justice are essentially comparative questions, though it has not gone uncontested, is one that is widely shared in modern social philosophy and policy. It implies that we must view any society as a whole in which the *pattern* of prosperity may be judged as just or unjust. It is an idea we shall have to examine at some length, but before that there is one final clarification on what social justice is not. Even if social justice is a pattern in the distribution of wealth, contrary to what is commonly supposed the proper pattern cannot be straightforward numerical equality. This is chiefly because of the abstractness of the idea of equality.

In any realistic social set-up where the justice of different distributions of wealth and power is to be assessed, there will almost always be a sizable number of different aspects in which cases may be treated equally or unequally. The story from the New Testament illustrates this. The workers were all paid an equal amount of money. But they had done unequal amounts of work. In fact their belief in this case was that an injustice had arisen precisely because they were improperly paid *equal* amounts. Even had they all worked and been paid the same amount, there might still be reason to think they were treated unequally since the value of the reward to each might be different – the less money you have the more valuable a little more will be, so that the value of a reward depends upon how well or badly off you already are.

Social justice, then, cannot be equality in any simple form. If we are to find a pattern in the distribution of wealth that coincides with justice it must arise from more complex principles. It is just such principles that we are offered in what is undoubtedly the most famous book in modern social and political philosophy – John Rawls's *A Theory of Justice*.

RAWLS AND JUSTICE

The Difference Principle

According to Rawls a well-ordered society, one that can commend itself to impartial critical scrutiny, will be ordered according to two principles. The first of these requires a society to allow the greatest possible liberty for the individual, compatible with a similar degree of liberty for all. This principle, obviously, is designed to capture and to express the value of a free society.

The second principle, which he calls 'the Difference Principle', is intended to capture the belief in the fundamental *equality* of all citizens. The equality it aims to realize, however, is of a substantial kind. It is not merely the right of all to secure their own interests as best they may, but the equal claim of all to a share in the wealth which a society produces. On Rawls's view, though, this does not mean that each has a claim to an equal share. There may indeed be considerable differences in the ownership of goods of various sorts within a society, so that some people are wealthy and others relatively poor, and yet the society may still be a just one. But it can only be just in as far as the disparities of wealth contribute to the greater benefit of the least well off. That is to say, a just society will allow people to accumulate great wealth only to the extent that this actually improves the lot of the poor, makes them better off than they would be if such differences in wealth were not permitted.

Rawls believes that conflict between the claims of individual liberty on the one hand and social justice on the other can be avoided by ordering the two principles 'lexically', and giving priority to the principle of liberty. What this means is that, on each occasion in any given context, we must first satisfy the principle of liberty, and only then the Difference Principle.

Finally, we should add that what makes these two the

principles of a well-ordered society is that it is such a society which any rational, self-interested person who considered the matter impartially would be happy to accept.

This very brief summary has omitted the arguments which Rawls brings in support of his contentions in the course of a long book. It would be impossible to examine them in detail in the space available here, in fact, but what we can do is to look at the space available here, in fact, but what we can do is to look at the arguments (and the objections to them) which have been shown to be important by the extensive discussion of *A Theory of Justice* that has taken place since the book was first published.

Objections to the Difference Principle

According to Rawls a just society would be one in which there is a limit to the extent to which one person can be better off than another. This limit is fixed by the requirement that the richest can only be as rich as is necessary to make the poorest as well off as they can be. Suppose that in some society the highest income is £500,000 per annum and and the lowest is £8000. There is thus an enormous gap between the richest and the poorest, but such a gap is permissible if, and only if, it is the case that were the highest income to be lower, the lowest income would be smaller too.

It will be very difficult in many cases to know whether as a matter of fact any such causal connection holds, whether, that is to say, it actually is the case that redistribution would sooner or later make the poorest poorer. But we can imagine with comparative ease the sort of story which, if it were true, *would* make the connection hold. Perhaps the entrepreneurs who receive this very large income would not work so hard, at securing export orders and so on, if they were limited to £450,000, and if they did not work so hard those who now have the lowest paid jobs would have no jobs at all and would be reduced to surviving on social security, which, let us suppose, would provide an income well below £8,000 per annum.

There are two important questions that must be asked of this, and of any conception of social justice: first, why we should accept it, and secondly, what makes it a conception of *justice* . It is one of the great attractions of Rawls's theory that its central idea combines answers to both these questions, because, according to the theory, what commends the Difference Principle is the fact that any self-interested but impartial reasoner would deem it an acceptable principle by which society should be governed (since it is based on rational self-interest) and that the same fact shows it to be just (since the reasoning is impartial).

Both these contentions have been questioned directly, but to my mind a greater weakness is in two assumptions which lie behind the theory, one about what it is rational to choose when faced with alternatives, and the other about what an impartially derived principle may properly be applied to. Both of these are dubious, but to appreciate these doubts we must look a little more closely into the argumentation by which Rawls supports his principles.

Rawls imagines that a group of people is asked to agree upon a set of social principles 'behind a veil of ignorance'. That is to say, they are asked to agree upon the sort of society they are willing to live in, without knowing anything about their own personal circumstances, without knowing whether they are clever or stupid, lazy or enterprising, talented or dull. This 'veil of ignorance' is intended to make sure that the principles the contracting parties agree upon are really impartial, for if they do not know precisely what or where they will be in the society they are about to enter, they cannot rig its principles to favour themselves. Under such conditions, Rawls believes that everyone would choose conservatively, that they would forego the chance to be enormously rich, should they turn out to be clever and enterprising, giving preference to the knowledge that they would not fall below a certain level, should they turn out to be lazy and stupid. This is known as the 'maximin' strategy, a strategy for choosing between possible outcomes under which it is rational to opt for the least worst outcome (the maximum minimum) rather than simply the best possible outcome.

But why should rationally self-interested agents be conservative in this way? If we imagine ourselves under a veil of ignorance, not knowing, that is to say, just what social position we are going to occupy and able to choose between societies organized on different principles, it seems just as rational to prefer the chance of fabulous wealth to the certainty of less than total poverty. This means that Rawls's argument rests upon an assumption that the contracting parties will be more fearful of poverty than they are desirous of wealth. Without this assumption, his argument does not produce the Difference Principle as its conclusion. But because this is an assumption about human dispositions, not about the principles of rationality itself, the argument does not show his Difference Principle to be uniquely rational, an argument that anyone, whatever their psychological make-up, has reason to accept. This means he has not shown this to be the only principle of social distribution we could rationally support.

It might be thought that this illicit assumption also destroys the impartiality of the reasoning, since it now appears to be a reasoning that favours one sort of person over another, namely those who dislike a gamble, and this is not a disposition that is universally shared. In fact the reasoning remains impartial: it's just that the people to whom it is applicable are limited. It is, if you like, impartial reasoning which does not apply universally, so that a more important question is: is the *impartiality* of the Difference Principle enough to show that any distribution in accordance with it is *just*?

There are reasons for thinking that it is not. Compare two different circumstances. In one we have to decide how a cake which we have all made should be divided up. Let us suppose that there is some way in which we can arrive at an impartial principle of distribution which it is rational for any and all of us to accept, a principle concerned with how much each contributed to the making of the cake, perhaps. We may then agree, when the cake is cut up in accordance with the application of this principle, that the resulting distribution is just. But compare this with another case in which thieves steal a cake and then deliberate upon the rational principle by which they should divide it among themselves. Again they arrive at a principle based upon the amount of effort each has contributed to its being stolen, and agree upon a principle which each of them has good reason to accept. But there seems no good reason to agree that the resulting distribution is just, even if it was arrived at in this way, since it overlooks a crucial difference between the two cases. In the first, the cake was ours to divide, in the second it was not theirs.

One way philosophers put this is to say that in the first case the cake is 'available for redistribution' in accordance with whatever principle we may agree upon, while in the second it is *not* available for redistribution, and so any principle of distribution agreed upon is irrelevant. Now Rawls assumes that, within the society which the contracting parties are about to form, all goods are available for redistribution, that the wealth which arises from the efforts of the talented or enterprising is available for redistribution to the talentless or lazy. But why should we accept this assumption? Indeed there seems positive reason not to.

Consider another New Testament story. A landowner goes away on a journey leaving each of his servants a certain sum of money. The sum in question is a 'talent' and it is from this story our own idea of 'talents' is derived. On his return he asks them to give him an account of what they have done with the talents they were left. It turns out that one servant has done nothing with his, but left it buried in the ground for fear that he would lose it. His master is extremely angry and has him punished, whereas those who made good use of the money they had been left in charge of are rewarded. The story assumes, as most of us do, that when it comes to the distribution of rewards at the end of a productive process, some account must be taken of the use that each has made of the goods with which he or she has begun. What this means is that the money which the servants have generated while their master is away cannot properly be thought of as a pool available for distribution amongst them according to some general principle. The generation of the pool brings with it differing rights to it, in accordance with the different contributions that have gone into its making.

But Rawls's Difference Principle ignores this. It supposes that the different talents and characteristics each of the hypothetical contracting parties brings to the society that together they will form will be a matter of no relevance to the way in which the resulting material benefits of their collaboration should be shared out. Actually, it is not quite right to say that the Difference Principle ignores this dimension of distributive justice. Rather it denies that it is an aspect of justice, because Rawls argues quite explicitly that the natural endowments of individuals, since they are not to be regarded as merits of that individual, should be regarded as nothing more than the outcome of a 'natural lottery'. In other words, there is no reason in justice to think that the clever should benefit from their cleverness more than those who are, through no fault of their own, less clever. And this contention, no less than the New Testament story, we should add, accords with what many people instinctively feel.

But I do not think that we can reasonably accept this view. To put the matter abstractly, if there is to be any distribution whatever, just or unjust, there must be *possessors* of the goods distributed and these possessors must have personal characteristics of some sort. But if that is so, we cannot deny the possibility that these characteristics may properly be used to benefit the possessor. Which characteristics count as personal in this sense, however, is something about which we may argue.

We may put the point less abstractly in this way. If we are to distribute goods at all, there must be individuals to whom they are distributed. How are these individuals to be distinguished one from another? Only, presumably, in terms of personal characteristics, things like being very musical, good with animals, hardworking, insightful and so on. Such characteristics are personal in the sense that, were we to strip the individual of them, as senile decay sometimes does, we should have altered the essential person. Other characteristics, let us agree, are not like this. These might include the colour of one's hair or skin. They bear no essential relation to the person, for were they to change, this would not be a change in personality. Still other characteristics we may be unsure about. Can a handsome man or beautiful woman, someone strong or someone weak, undergo change in these respects without becoming a different person? People have quite different intuitions about many of these and consequently disagree. But that there must be *some* essentially personal characteristics if there is to be a person at all seems certain.

Such characteristics may bring their own benefits, however. The owner of stables may succeed chiefly through a talent for dealing with horses, the engineer may prosper through an ingenuity without which he or she would be a quite different person, and so on. If, then, we treat these benefits as accidental to the person from whose essential characteristics they flow, we have lost a very fundamental sense in which things belong to people. If from my musicality a symphony springs, it seems incontestable that it is *my* composition. If we deny this, and suppose that, although it was an expression of my essential musicality, it is nonetheless the property of the community as a whole, we have denied a mode of ownership so fundamental that there now seems no reason to think that individuals can own things at all. But if so, what reason is there to hold that the things allocated to them by the Difference Principle belong to them either?

Another way of putting the same point is to say that, even in a society set up in the way that Rawls imagines, at least some goods and benefits will come into existence with claims attached, and cannot therefore be treated as common property available for general redistribution. This way of putting it, in fact, is to be found in one of Rawls's best known critics, Robert Nozick. But in his book *Anarchy, State, and Utopia*, Nozick does not simply criticize Rawls. He also offers a positive account of social justice himself. Since his account is founded on a recognition of the point that we have just criticized Rawls for ignoring, this seems an appropriate place to turn to it.

NOZICK AND THE HISTORICAL THEORY OF SOCIAL JUSTICE

Nozick's theory of the state and of social justice draws upon John Locke's conception, discussed in the first chapter. Locke, it will be recalled, imagines a world in which there is no state or legal system, and asks what rights people would have in such a condition. One of the rights he thinks they would have is a right to private property. For, since at the outset in this pre-political world no one owns anything, everyone has an equal right to everything. What makes something mine and something else yours, then? Locke's answer is that it is mine if I expended labour upon it in appropriating it, that is, taking it out of common ownership and into my own possession. The idea is a very simple one. If we are walking across a piece of common land and you see an interestingly shaped stick, there is, at this point, no reason for us to call the stick yours, which is to say that I have as much right to it as you do. But if you pick it up and with the help of a knife enhance its interest and appearance, whereas I walk on by, there is, after this point, good reason to call the stick yours and deny that I have any right to it at all. What this means is that in a purely natural condition there would, despite the absence of any institutional legal authority, be rights to private property. And consequently there would be items of property which it would be a violation of right, an injustice, to take away.

There is more to Locke's theory than this, and indeed more to the use that Nozick makes of it, but enough has been said to show how Nozick arrives at his own theory of social justice. If in a world without pre-existing laws, we simply reflect on what would be reasonable conduct, we can see that freely doing what you want with what you have as much right to as anyone else generates a right of private property. This is to say that independently of any legal system there can be justice and injustice in the matter of possessions, or 'holdings' as Nozick calls them. Now if, as a matter of fact, everyone in a given society has come by their possessions justly, then the distribution of possessions in that society will be just. If it is the case that I came by my possessions justly and thus have a right to them, you came by yours justly and thus have a right to them, she came by hers justly, and so on, then things are as they should be from the point of view of distributive justice.

Justice and history

But of course this means that the crucial question we must ask about the distribution of possessions within a society is not what the overall pattern is like, but how it came about, because there is no reason to think that individuals freely engaged on their own affairs in wholly legitimate ways – buying, selling, swapping, giving, bequeathing – will end up owning things according to some preordained pattern.

This in fact is Nozick's objection to nearly all familiar conceptions of social justice, that they impose a pattern of ownership and call it 'just', without inquiring how it came about, and yet how it came about is, if we think about it, crucial to the question of its justice.

This criticism plainly applies to the pattern which would

result from the application of Rawls's Difference Principle just as much as the application of any other abstract patterning principle, for instance Marx's famous suggestion that the principle of distributing social burdens and benefits should be 'from each according to his abilities, to each according to his needs'. Any such principle, Nozick thinks, is mistaken because it is deeply ahistorical; it takes no account of how things came about. But he has a second and related point to make. Precisely because they are ahistorical such principles of social justice must be in conflict with the freedom of the individual.

To see this we have only to imagine a world in which things are distributed according to an acceptable-looking principle, similar to Rawls's. Following the distribution, however, individuals would use the goods they were entitled to under the principle quite differently – some would squander them, others give them away, others invest them in money-making schemes, still others simply lose them – so that after almost any length of time the pattern of ownership established by the original principle would have been disrupted. If, for example, everyone had been given the same amount of money, pretty soon, by buying, giving, bequeathing and so on, people would have *different* amounts of money. To say that the pattern ought to be re-established, however, would be the same as saying that individuals ought not to have been allowed freely to do what they wanted with what was, according to the principle, their own, and this is tantamount to saying that, in the interests of social justice (so conceived) individuals ought not to be free.

This argument, it seems to me, is a good one and its conclusion sound. But even so, it does not provide us with a knock-down argument against principled conceptions of social justice. Over the years many socialists (and others) have accepted, even argued, that unbridled freedom, chiefly in the market place, will lead to widespread social injustice as they conceive it. But far from thinking this an objection to their conception of justice, they have, in the name of a just society, argued for limitations on the freedom of the individual. Nozick would respond, of course, by asking what it is they think makes the inequalities that result from freedom *injustices*, for if they have come about by fair means, there is no injustice. But to this response the convinced socialist has a reply also, namely that the injustice of the resulting inequalities lies in their being contrary to a principle of justice – perhaps a revised version of Rawls's Difference Principle – on which any rational self-interested agent would agree.

In other words, Nozick's argument about freedom produces stalemate rather than victory, and for this reason he must rely upon the first point, the historical nature of social justice, to establish his case. But it is here in fact that the greatest weakness of his theory lies.

Objections to the historical conception of social justice

If we suppose, and Nozick has given us good reason to do so, that justice is a backward-looking concept, one which requires us to look not just into how things stand but how they came about, we will have to agree at once that whether or not the distribution of material wealth and other benefits across a society is just is a matter of its history. To inquire into social justice, therefore, is to inquire into the past, and to be an enthusiast for social justice will be a matter of rectifying past injustices rather than bringing about some egalitarian pattern on non-historical grounds.

But once we have seen this, we are able to see also that the prospect of actually doing this for any real society is slim indeed. In the first place, the relevant history of most societies is, for the most part, unknown. Just imagine trying to discover the ownership history of every good and artefact in a society of any complexity. Even in a modern society with good historical records, the task is impossibly difficult, but in societies with few or no records (which is to say almost all societies before 1500) it would be absurd even to try to undertake it. Yet this is what we are required to do if we are to establish which things are justly held by which people.

It might be objected that all the theory requires us to do is to determine and to uphold just possession in those cases where we *do* know the relevant history. Admittedly, if these cases are limited in number the historical theory of social justice loses some of its initial attraction, but the absence of relevant historical knowledge cannot show the theory to be false, or that it has no application.

If ignorance were all there were to it, such defence of the
theory would be correct. But in fact the difficulties are greater
than we have so far made them out to be. This is because in
many cases the history of possessions, when it is known, far
from settling present questions of justice makes them more
difficult still.

For example, suppose that I am rich, the owner of a
prosperous chain of stores, and you are poor, having had
difficulty in securing employment because of a poor education.
Suppose further that the chain of stores bears your name
because the business with which it began belonged to your
great-grandfather. But he was cheated out of it by his
unscrupulous manager, my great-grandfather, and while your
once well-to-do family sank lower and lower, my once humble
family rose higher and higher. Do you have a right, according
to the historical theory of social justice, to a share of my
business? At first sight the answer would appear to be 'yes',
since there is injustice in the history of the business I own. But
actually the answer is not as plain as this. There may be no
reason to think that your grandfather, had he inherited the
business as expected, would have brought to the business the
drive, imagination and talent which my grandfather brought to
the business he unexpectedly inherited, a business admittedly
stolen by his father. In fact, there may even be reason to think
that, in the hands of your grandfather, a well-known wastrel,
the business would have gone under. If so, you would be no
better off now, very likely, than you are given the earlier theft.

Where this sort of thing is true, there is no reason to suppose
that the historical actuality of the theft calls for any redistribution of wealth between you and me. If you are no worse off
now than you would have been without that injustice, what is
there to rectify by redistribution? There is, of course, the
injustice itself, but that was committed by someone who is dead
against someone who is dead, not by me against you, and
cannot therefore be rectified by me to you. I cannot make good
the injustices of the past except in so far as they may properly be
held responsible for injustices in the present.

This imaginary example is relatively simple. Consider a real
case. When Europeans moved across what is now the mid-west
of the United States they made treaties with the Indians who

lived there, trading land for goods of one sort or another. Many of the bargains they made were unfair, or relied upon their ability to dupe the Indians, but on the other hand, since private ownership of land was virtually unknown, it is unclear that those Indian chiefs who concluded such bargains had any right to do so. In any event the treaties were broken by the governments of the white settlers, sometimes on feeble grounds, sometimes on relatively good grounds, so that the pattern of ownership that was finally established had little to do with the just transfer of justly acquired property. There is no doubt, however, that the waves of settlers who arrived in the mid-west, often in an effort to escape persecution in Europe, extracted from the land wealth far in excess of anything the Indians would have done. From this new wealth some Indians benefited, but most were excluded until whole tribes became drunken paupers. In recent years taxes have been used to make generous payments to the descendants of those Indians, but as this brief outline suggests, whatever the merits of such payments, the history is too complex to allow us to regard them as rectifications required by the historical theory of justice. If distributive justice is involved it cannot be justice derived from a knowledge of the relevant history.

What this sort of example shows is that even when we know the history of present possessions, we may still be unable to apply the historical theory of justice, because what its implications are in cases of any moral complexity remains quite uncertain.

This leaves us with the following alternatives: either we abandon the historical theory, or we abandon the pursuit of social justice. The first of these does not seem wholly acceptable. After all, it is indeed true that, given just acquisition and a history of just transfer, the result must be just whatever pattern of possession has emerged. To adopt principles like those which Rawls offers us, therefore, is to adopt a system of distribution which may well bring about injustices. And this, if it is justice that is supposed to be motivating us, can hardly be acceptable. In other words, though the theory can hardly ever, perhaps never, actually tell us when social justice prevails, it still seems to be an accurate account of justice. Should we then abandon the pursuit of social justice on the grounds that, though we know what it would be, we can never tell when we have it?

Such a conclusion is too swift. In fact there are contexts in which questions of social justice arise which the historical theory could not *in principle* settle, and where, consequently, Rawls-type principles might still be of some use. It is to these we should now turn.

SOCIAL JUSTICE AND SOCIAL CO-OPERATION

The historical theory we have just been considering, though it has been interestingly revitalized by Nozick, has its origins in Locke's *Second Treatise*, for it is really an extension of Locke's theory of the right to private property. Whatever the merits of this theory, and over the years it has come in for a good deal of criticism, any extension of it to the subject of social justice makes two assumptions about the goods which principles of social justice seek to distribute – first that they are goods to which initially individuals have an equal title (what Locke calls goods held in common), and secondly that, once an individual has appropriated them justly, he or she has an absolute claim to them. Now we can think of systems of property of which this is true. For instance, consider what makes a drink at a party *mine*. Initially, all drinks are held in common, that is to say, they are provided by the host or hostess equally for everyone invited. Individual guests 'appropriate' a drink to their exclusive use by labour – in this case the 'labour' of lifting it from a tray, or pouring it out. The principle of distribution here is basically historical – whether a drink is mine or not is a matter or how it came to be where it is.

But rather obviously such a principle, as Locke himself saw, is not sufficient on its own to govern the behaviour of party-goers. Should I spend the first fifteen minutes of the party pouring all the gin into glasses, this is not enough to make them all my drinks. Since there is no reason to think that in justice, or for any other reason, *I* ought to have all the gin, we need to add to the historical entitlement theory the proviso that, in general, individual appropriation must leave 'enough and as good' for others (as Locke puts it).

Though it seems reasonable enough, there are in fact problems about this proviso. Does it mean, to continue the party example, that no one can ever justly help themselves to the last drink? If so, it begins to seem less reasonable. But any such problems are less important than the fact that there are circumstances in which the proviso does not seem to apply. These are circumstances in which the first assumption of the Lockean theory – that initially goods are held in common – is false. At the party, initially the drinks *are* held in common just in the sense that they are available to any guest. But in other contexts individuals bring valuable goods into existence, and it seems wrong to think that such goods are, or ever could be, available to all equally. They are rather, from the first moment of their existence, the property of some one individual. For example, if I compose an attractive theme tune which several television companies want to use, I have no need to 'appropriate' this valuable item, justly or unjustly. It is mine from the word go, so to speak.

This is not an objection to Nozick. It is in fact a point he himself makes. Its importance is this. The historical theory of justice says that what I make my own out of the common stock is justly mine, regardless of what others make their own. But the proviso about leaving enough and as good for others shows this to be false. I can legitimately labour upon the common stock and fail to make things mine if others have, by my labour, been deprived. But this is true only where, as in the party example, there is something which we may regard as a common stock of goods. Where there are goods, like the theme tune, which are *never* in any sense part of a common stock, the individual cannot justly be deprived of them. This means that, though principles of the type Rawls offers us may have a role to play in establishing which appropriation from a common stock might justly be regulated, they cannot be applied to those cases where individual wealth creation takes place. Since the creation of wealth by individuals may result in gross disparities between them, this means that Rawls-type principles cannot be applied quite generally to the distribution of goods within a society.

Goods that come into existence by the wealth-creating activities of individuals, then, do not seem proper objects for social redistribution. This is, I think, the main force of Nozick's objection to Rawls. But not all goods are in fact of this sort. Most important, perhaps, of those that are not are goods which arise from co-operative endeavour.

Justice and the co-operative generation of wealth

Consider the following case. A group of people get together to build a bridge across a river. This bridge will bring great advantages in terms of trade, agriculture and general conveni-ence. It will, in short, be a highly valuable creation, so that its building will be an act of wealth creation. But it cannot be built by one person alone. No one has the combination of talents, strength and dexterity to do the job, and of course people get together to do it for mutual advantage. Now it is obvious that different sorts and amounts of labour will go into it, besides, perhaps, materials previously belonging to individuals.

Once the bridge is built the question arises as to how the resulting wealth is to be distributed. The historical theory suggests, rightly, that any just distribution must take account of how the bridge came to be built and the relative burdens that were borne in its building. But it is obvious that, however it is to be applied, the theory cannot result in a straightforward allocation of parts of the bridge. In the first place the value lies in the bridge as a whole – what each person wants is use of the bridge, not ownership of some of its parts – and in the second place, that association with some one part of the bridge is precisely what *co-operative* endeavour makes impossible. If it took three of us pulling on a rope to secure part of the bridge in place, there is no reason to allocate any third of anything to anyone.

What we have encountered is the problem of distributing *socially* as opposed to *individually* generated benefits (and burdens) justly, and we have seen that no straightforward application of the historical theory could settle this for us, even in principle. It might be suggested, however, that the historical principle can settle this sort of case in a less straightforward way. Consider the bridge again. Suppose a group of entre-preneurs should see the desirability of the bridge, and, despite general scepticism, freely contract with all the necessary traders at agreed rates of pay, undertaking the financial risk themselves should the venture fail. In fact, however, it is a tremendous success, and, having paid all the traders, the entrepreneurs become extremely wealthy on the bridge-tolls that they collect. In this case, the proponent of the historical theory will argue, the relevant history includes the history of bargains transacted, and once this is clear, the just distribution of the new wealth *is* clear.

It is this view which underlies the belief that in the first story taken from the New Testament there is no injustice, that the labourers hired from the first hour of the day have no complaint against the distribution of rewards, since they freely agreed to the terms of their employment and those terms have been kept. Of course they may well be *envious* of the workers taken on in the last hour, but there is no reason to think that justice must coincide with their envy. Similarly, the entrepreneurs who built the bridge have a just entitlement to their new found wealth, however great, because every one involved in the building of the bridge freely agreed to terms which were kept. If now they are envious of the entrepreneurs' wealth, this gives us no reason in justice to secure part of it for them, a conclusion which holds equally well even if, being more numerous, they are politically more powerful and the redistribution takes place through a system of taxation.

Where this is the case, it seems to me, the historical theorist is right. Those who freely agree upon the terms of a contract cannot justly insist upon benefits other than those to which the contract entitles them, however productive their efforts may have turned out to be. But two points need to be made about this conclusion. First, as many socialists in the past have pointed out, this conclusion says nothing about what is properly considered a case of 'freely' contracting. It is easy to discover circumstances in which most incomes are low and a local manufacturer has a monopoly of employment opportunities, so that workers have no choice but to contract 'freely' to work at wage rates over which they have virtually no control. Indeed it was the existence of such circumstances which led many free-trade liberals to agree to the regulatory activities of wage boards and the like. Where such conditions exist, there seems no good reason to be overimpressed by the mere existence of a contract, and this includes not being unduly impressed when it comes to sharing out the profits which the factory makes.

Such an objection to the operations of the so-called free market is well known. It is not, however, a very important objection in the present context, because what we want to know for the purposes of the theory of social justice is whether, in circumstances where there really is freedom of contract, the historical theory of social justice is the right one to adopt. And though we shall have to return to the matter of freedom of contract, the answer is 'no', because very few cases of co-operative wealth creation are or actually could be of this kind. This point needs to be considered in more detail, but before we do so a summary of the objections we have discovered to the historical theory of social justice might be useful.

Summary

At bottom the historical theory rests upon the idea that it is the history of transactions between individuals and of their causal contributions to wealth creation that are important to distributive justice. This is an intuitively appealing idea with which it is hard to quarrel, and precisely for this reason any purely patterning principle, like Rawls's Difference Principle, which concerns itself only with contemporary patterns of relative wealth between individuals and ignores the different roles they may have played in the acquistion and creation of that wealth, seems quite unacceptable. This has led some people to the false conclusion that history is everything and that any redistribution by way of taxation, other than compensation for theft, fraud and the like, is unjustifiable and could only appear to be justified in the abstract visions of the extreme egalitarian.

But this is wrong. We have seen, first, that the history of wealth creation and acquisition may be unknown to us and hence valueless as a guide to social justice; or if known it may be of a very mixed moral character, and hence allow us to pass no clear judgement on the justice or injustice of any proposed or existing schemes for the redistribution of wealth. Secondly we have seen that in the case of the creation of wealth, history could *not* be the whole story, since in some cases, at least, a limit on how much wealth any one individual may justly acquire relative to other people seems reasonable. This means that on occasions the pattern of possession *will* be sufficient to tell us that something is wrong. Thirdly, it has emerged further that where wealth is created through the co-operative endeavour of a number of people, there is no obvious connection between the individual's part in its creation and his or her share in its benefits.

Faced with the suggestion that the history of free contractual relations will settle questions about who should receive what, then, we can observe that this is true only in a very small number of cases.

Distributing co-operatively generated wealth

Consider once more the bridge example, this time with a further modification. Let us suppose that the demand for a road across the river, which brings the builders great wealth, arises from the invention of cars, an invention unforeseen by the entrepreneurs. Of course, it is still true that without their foresight, imagination and drive the bridge would not have been built, and that they paid the various traders in accordance with agreements freely arrived at. But had the car-generated demand been foreseen, the rates they would have had to agree to would undoubtedly have been much higher. The unexpected demand certainly makes the entrepreneurs' activity more productive than was anticipated, but by the same token it makes the activity of *all* those whose services were involved in the building of the bridge unexpectedly more productive. The resulting wealth is, certainly, wealth that could only arise because of the bridge, but this does not mean that it is wealth exclusively earned by the people who thought of the bridge; it is wealth that has, through chance, accrued to the activities of all those involved in building the bridge. There seems no reason, therefore, why the entrepreneurs should benefit exclusively from it.

Now something of this sort is true of nearly every product invented or made in a society of any complexity. Bright ideas flourish best in a world where there is educated labour, a discriminating market, and widespread technical innovation.

None of these things are under the control of the entrepreneur, however, though they all make important contributions to the success of the entrepreneur's schemes. This raises consequential questions of justice. If I teach computing well, do I deserve a share in the wealth of the inventor whose technological successes depend upon being able to recruit computer operators who have been well taught? If I show drive, initiative and imagination as a publisher of books, do those who have laboured for years to raise the level of adult literacy have no claim to any of my wealth? At the very least, the answer to these questions is unclear. And it is unclear precisely in so far as we are persuaded by the historical theory of social justice. It is precisely because it seems plausible to hold that a great many people have had a hand in the creation of the entrepreneur's wealth that thoughts of redistribution from the entrepreneur to them seem reasonable. Such redistribution would be just, it might be argued, because it would amount to giving the rewards of industry to those who were due them. Add to this the important practical consideration that, though we must in justice acknowledge the contribution made by society in general to the success of the imaginative individual, there seems little practical prospect of breaking this down into individual contributions. This implies that the best we can hope for is a *general* system of redistribution which will ensure that everyone gets a reasonably fair share of the rewards that living in society brings.

We have only to add that any system of fair distribution must not discourage the sort of initiative that serves to make us all better off for it to seem that we have come full circle and are back with Rawls's Difference Principle, according to which we may permit only those differences in wealth that are necessary to make the poorest as well off as they can be. Does this mean that Rawls is right, after all?

JUSTICE AND FREEDOM

One of the main objections to patterning principles of the kind Rawls offers us is that they allow the possibility that free interaction among autonomous agents (people who know what they're doing, and are doing what they have a perfect right to do) may result in social injustice, while it is the chief attraction of the historical theory that it makes this impossible. For on the historical view the free society *is* a just one. It might seem, on the strength of the objections just considered, however, that this is not so, that a perfectly free society is incompatible with a just one and that, as socialists have frequently maintained, the unbridled activities of self-interested individuals will always lead to inequalities and injustices.

But behind this doubt lies a way of thinking expressed most famously, perhaps, by the eighteenth-century political philosopher Jean Jacques Rousseau, who wrote at the beginning of his *Social Contract* 'Man is born free but everywhere he is in chains'; the chains, that is to say, of laws and social institutions. In other words, the natural or original human condition is one of freedom, and the social condition one of enslavement. Viewed in this way, the problem of social philosophy is the problem of justifying unfreedom, and one justification might be that social constraints are needed for the sake of social justice. But in fact this way of looking at the ideal of freedom in which an individualist believes is one we saw reason to abandon in an earlier chapter. We should not think of the free society as a natural condition which laws and institutions at best are used to preserve, but as an ideal yet to come which good laws and institutions might help to realize. This means that even though we can see the limitations of a simple historical conception of social justice, we must not therefore rest content with the alternative conception which construes it as a necessary constraint on freedom, but rather proceed to ask what conception of society would enable us to realize both justice and freedom.

The answer is a society in which socially generated benefits and burdens are distributed as far as possible according to the free contracts of individuals pursuing their own interests. This acknowledges the fundamental perception of the historical theory that the just creation and acquisition of goods must result in a just distribution and that it is a mistake to try to impose some preconceived and abstract pattern of social justice, irrespective of the activities of wealth creating and acquiring individuals. But at the same time it leaves us scope to take account of the various objections to the historical theory we have considered, chiefly that unforeseen events, limited resources, and inequalities between contracting parties can produce circumstances in which any straightforward application of the idea of 'freely contracting parties' is bound to lead to injustice. What this means, though, is not that the historical conception of social justice is intrinsically at fault, or that the freedom of individuals is incompatible with justice, but that in the contingent circumstances of the world we actually inhabit it may well be necessary to create conditions of freedom, often through laws and social policies.

One of these conditions is material prosperity. We saw that the requirement to leave 'enough and as good for others' puts a constraint on the freedom of the individual in the acquisition of limited resources, just as the total quantity of wine at a party limits the number of glasses I can pour myself. This constraint can be lifted, of course, by an increase in those resources, and this explains the relation between freedom, justice and the pursuit of prosperity, though just how prosperity should be promoted and what the role of the state in wealth creation should be is a difficult subject in its own right.

But behind the idea that justice must result from free interaction between autonomous parties lies an important assumption, the assumption of social equality between the two parties. Nobody supposes that a belief in freedom of contract requires us to uphold the 'contract' between a child and an adult whereby the child gains a bag of marbles in return for his or her life interest in a large estate, and this is because of the inequality of the contracting parties. But at the same time we must acknowledge that there *can* be contracts which result in equally serious disadvantages to one of the parties, but which justice requires us to uphold. The essential difference is not in the *outcome* (which, let us suppose, is much the same in money terms) but in the conditions under which each contract was made, so that justice resides not in some approximation to equality in the result, but in equality of a relevant kind in the conditions under which free activity is engaged in. Given this initial equality, the free creation, acquisition and transfer of wealth *is* guaranteed to be just whatever the pattern of its outcome. What justice requires, then, is some measure of social equality not as a *supplement to* but as a *condition of* freedom, and in so far as laws and social policies promote equality in this regard and for this reason they will be promoting the free society and the just society simultaneously. This brings us to the subject of social equality.

4

Social Equality and Affirmative Action

We have seen that a free society is one in which individuals are as free as possible to pursue their own interests, and further that such a society, in theory at least, is not merely compatible with a just society, but identical with it. This is because in such a society there is no one distributor of socially generated burdens and benefits – such things as taxes, military service, jail sentences on the one hand, and earnings, medical care, civil and military protection on the other. The distribution of these things – who has what and how much – arises from the interaction of autonomous agents freely pursuing their own interests as they think fit (which, let it always be remembered, must not be taken to mean the selfish pursuit of self-serving interests). Since in such circumstances, there can be nothing to complain about from the point of view of rights, wrongs and entitlements, this result must be just even though it may not, perhaps is unlikely to, give the individuals concerned *equal* amounts of the relevant burdens and benefits. In fact, it may not even comply with the requirements of Rawls's two principles, according to which, it will be remembered, no one can be richer than that it takes to make the poorest as well off as they can be. But we can still regard it as a socially just distribution, because it has come about in the right way. Moreover, any attempt, on the part of the state say, to interfere with it would have to be based on considerations of equality or need or desert in the abstract, and none of these, we saw at the beginning of the last chapter, will provide a proper basis for justice.

But the identity of the free and the just society holds only under certain conditions, notably that of equality between individuals in their dealings one with another, for if there is a sufficient degree of *in*equality we cannot hold exchanges between individuals to be free in the proper sense.

What sort of equality is this, and how does it differ from the equality which thoroughgoing egalitarian conceptions of social justice require? Those dying of thirst are not in a good position to bargain with the well-fed water seller, but this does not of itself mean their freedom is impaired. The difference is sometimes expressed as a difference between a belief in equality of *opportunity* and equality of *outcome*. This, as we shall see, is not quite the right way of putting the difference, but it is at any rate a good place to start.

Equality of opportunity v. equality of outcome

Think of a game of Monopoly. At the start everyone has the same amount of money and the same chance of buying any of the properties, and everyone is dependent upon the throw of the dice and bound by the same rules. There is in these respects equality between the players at the start of the game. But of course there is a decided inequality at the end. Some will be bankrupt and no longer in the game at all and others will be left propertyless and with little money while some one player takes nearly everything. It is tempting to describe the matter thus: although not every player wins, each has an equal opportunity to win. And it is tempting to add that even though the end result is one of gross inequality between players, the initial condition of equal opportunity for all players makes the game fair.

The moment we describe it in this way, however, doubts and questions arise. What does equal opportunity amount to? Two lines of thought suggest themselves, one having to do with the equality of the conditions under which the game is played, the other with there simply being some conditions at the start. On the first point the game of Monopoly presents few difficulties, because it involves so little skill (though it is instructive to note here that adults generally find it easy to beat children), but in other games it is much more obvious that an initial equality of material resources would be an inadequate basis upon which to secure true equality of opportunity. In golf, for instance, it is not enough to provide every player with equally good clubs;

some system of handicapping is also needed, and the idea behind this is that equality of opportunity must take account not merely of external conditions, but of internal factors also, such as the relative skill of the competitors. And of course, when we turn from games to social life in general, we can see at once that this line of thought readily makes way for the suggestion that, if there is to be real equality of opportunity in society, steps must be taken to ensure that these 'internal' differences between people are taken into account. This might be done by providing different levels of social support – such as schooling and medical care – for different people. But how does this differ from straightforward equalizing in the distribution of goods, which is to say, equalizing outcomes as well as opportunities?

One reply is that a belief in equality of opportunity only requires us to equalize resources at the start, whereas a belief in equality as such requires us to equalize outcomes over and over again. An immediate problem with this is that social life, unlike golf or Monopoly, does not *have* a start, but even in the case of games an argument might be made for thinking that equalizing cannot legitimately be restricted to the outset and may properly be incorporated at later stages of the game. So, if there is indeed good reason to think that Monopoly should *begin* by giving everyone an equal opportunity to win, it is difficult to see why there should not be a similar sort of reason for thinking that everyone who reaches a later stage in the game should not have this equal opportunity to win restored. Indeed some games do this. In knock-out whist, for example, any player who survives any early round, by however slender a margin, begins the next round on a par with everyone else.

The parallel with social life is not hard to discern. If there is an argument for thinking that individuals should begin on an equal footing, there seems to be scope for equally convincing argument in favour of putting them on an equal footing again from time to time. And if we agree with this we have agreed to as ambitious a programme of intervention and redistribution as any enthusiastic egalitarian has ever wanted.

What this means is that radical interference in the distribution of burdens and benefits which individuals, left to their own devices, have brought about seems quite compatible with the historical individualist theory of social justice. And if so, this appears to imply first that even the revised and expanded historical theory can offer no guidance on what to do about actual distributions of wealth, and secondly that the dispute about conceptions of social justice between individualists and communitarians is no dispute at all.

Equality for freedom

To solve this puzzle it will prove instructive to look again at the structure of games, though in due course something will have to be said about the appropriateness of this analogy.

In a game, we saw, certain preconditions apply, the purpose of which is to secure for players an equal opportunity of winning. This does not necessarily mean an equal *chance* of winning, however, for in games of skill the differing abilities of the players will determine, and are meant to determine, the relative chances of winning. A better player has a higher chance of winning, and this is how it is supposed to be. What the conditions aim to do is to put the contestants on a roughly equal footing at the start (which we might call ensuring an initial material equality) and to treat them fairly as the contest proceeds (something we may call ensuring procedural justice). Now while we might suppose that procedural justice is required simply by a sense of justice itself, something which most games players feel keenly, the value of initial material equality is not *intrinsic* (valued for its own sake), but *instrumental* (valued for the results it has). The point of trying to ensure it is to allow the players to display qualities within them which are important *from the point of view of the game*.

This point needs to be emphasized. An eye for a ball or a strong right arm are properties of individuals which they may exploit and develop, but which they are not originally responsible for. Such things are, in religious language, *gifts*, not earnings, and it is with this thought in mind that thinkers like Rawls have come to the view that the material benefits of natural endowments are not uniquely the rightful property of the individual with those endowments. The individual's gifts are, after all and leaving aside religious conceptions, only a matter of chance. And once one starts thinking along these lines it is easy to be led to the view that the distribution of tennis prizes, say, is unjust, since it reflects not the merits but merely the inborn natural attributes of the players. But as we saw earlier, this is a mistake, for it strips the individual of *everything* that might make *her* the person *she* is. Moreover, even if we were to take the view that physical skills are implausible candidates for individual traits and cannot be considered essential to personality in the way that determination, intelligence and so on are (all of which may also bring material benefits), we would still have to allow that from the point of view of tennis, these just are the skills that matter, and *must* be thought of as essential to the players themselves, even if for other purposes we may have reason to regard them as mere physical attributes, arbitrarily distributed in what is sometimes called the natural lottery. The point to grasp is that if we are to play games like tennis and are to have winners and losers, the rules must be fashioned in the service of certain skills which are taken to be, in the strongest sense, essential to those who play.

It is these skills that are important. The immediate aim of a game is generally of no value in itself. Snooker players are not people who derive a peculiar satisfaction from the physical event of coloured balls disappearing into cloth pockets. What is satisfying about snooker is the test of skill that is uniquely involved in it. But it should be evident that there is little to be said *in general* about the abilities and aptitudes involved in the skilful playing of different games, for these will vary from game to game and activity to activity. Furthermore, the rules of different games and activities will themselves vary in accordance with the skills relevant to the game in question, and, indeed, with changing perceptions of how best to focus upon those skills. As a consequence, the immediate rationale of each game rests upon the relation between the rules and the skills for which it is played, while the ultimate rationale of any game will reside in the simple but profoundly important fact that human beings derive satisfaction from exploiting, developing and testing such skills in themselves and others.

What is the relevance of this to social rules and purposes? If what has been said of games is true, it follows that the sort of equality that exists between players is of two sorts. First there is the equality that derives from the impartial application of the rules. This is what I earlier called procedural justice, and its counterpart in social life is called 'equality before the law', a value often expressed in the legal principle that 'Like cases should be treated alike'. Such equality is crucial to the fair application of law, and is to be valued in itself. But of course it carries no necessary implications for material equality. Indeed it is most easily stated against a background of material *inequality*, since the whole point of equality before the law is that it is equality for rich and poor, high and low.

The second sort of equality in games is material equality between the players. This, we have seen, is *not* valuable in itself, but valuable for the part it plays in the promotion of the skills and attributes for which games are played. The parallel point to make about society at large, then, is that, contrary to the implication of conceptions of social justice considered earlier, material equality is to be valued not in itself but for its ability to promote the sorts of thing that social life is valued for. And, assuming the truth of the individualism explored in earlier chapters, this means that material equality is to be valued in so far, but only in so far, as it promotes individual autonomy.

Summary

We have seen that social justice must be conceived historically, that is to say, as a distribution of socially generated burdens and benefits whose justice or injustice lies not in the overall pattern of the distribution, but in how it has come about. To conclude this, however, is not to conclude that social equality has no part in social justice, or that redistribution of goods, perhaps by the coercive power of the state, is never required by social justice. A distribution is just according to its history, but this history must take into account the relative positions of the parties whose history it is.

One way in which this is often expressed is by saying that social justice requires not material equality or equality of outcome, but equality of opportunity. But we have seen that such a distinction is very hard to draw, because the difference between opportunity and outcome appears to be merely a difference in how the same thing is viewed. What may appear to be equality in the outcome of one activity can without difficulty or distortion be shown to be equality of opportunity for the next.

The analysis of games, however, shows that there *is* an important difference between two sorts of equality, the sort of equality which is involved in procedural justice, or equality before the law, and material equality of abilities or possessions. The difference is that, while the former is to be valued in itself as a constituent of justice, the latter is valuable only in so far as it serves other purposes. Equality of opportunity, in other words, is an unhappy expression which tries to capture a difference, not between two sorts of equality, but between material equality valued for its own sake and material equality valued for the purposes it serves.

In the second case, the value of material equality is instrumental and arises from the value of the end which it promotes. In the case of social equality this end, if the arguments about individualism have been sound, must be the autonomy of the individual. One way of putting such a conclusion to the test is to examine it in the context of attempts to produce social equality in some particular respect, and to see whether the best arguments for such a programme are those which defend it in terms of results for autonomy. Let us then examine one such example – affirmative action programmes.

AFFIRMATIVE ACTION

Social equality and unfair discrimination

We saw in a previous section that to have an equal opportunity (in the relevant sense) for the acquisition of some benefit is not the same as having an equal chance of obtaining it. This is a point not always easy to grasp. Two people bidding at an auction may have an equal opportunity to buy the the item under the hammer, but if they have different amounts of money at their disposal the probability of success is quite different for each of them. People often think that this second inequality negates the first, and that the poorer person at the auction does *not* have an opportunity equal to that of the wealthier. But, even though it may be true that, in ordinary English, talk of equality of opportunity is open to this interpretation, we must not overlook a very important difference between two sorts of case just because ordinary language is imprecise. For the case of the bidder with less money is quite different from that of someone whose bid is refused because he or she is Jewish.

What is the difference? The difference is that the poorer person's inability to pay more is relevant to what an auction is all about in a way that the Jew's Jewishness is not. We need to say more about it, of course, but there is no reason why we should not mark this important difference by saying that there is equality of opportunity for everyone engaged in some activity (even if they do not all have an equal chance of success) if the grounds upon which the distribution of burdens and benefits is decided, whether by private individuals or public officials, are those that are strictly relevant to the business in hand.

Why should we want equality of opportunity defined in this way? We will get a clue to the answer if we think of the auction again. The point of an auction is to bring together buyers and sellers in a mutually satisfactory financial relationship. Sellers will be rightly dissatisfied if the price they obtain is less than they could have obtained had the auction been more efficiently run. And of course if there are arbitrary exclusions which prevent the wealthiest from bidding, this is just what will happen. Discrimination on grounds of religion or nationality may be relevant from many other points of view, but from the point of view of the auction these grounds are quite irrelevant.

One implication of this is that, contrary to common usage, there is nothing wrong with discrimination in itself. Indeed we all *ought* to discriminate between good and bad in auction bids, appointments to jobs, sporting competitions and almost everything else. What is objectionable is *unfair* discrimination, discrimination based upon irrelevant considerations.

But this should not be taken to imply that discrimination must always be strictly relevant to the activity in hand if it is not to be unfair or improper. There is no reason to think that auctioneers, for instance, must be limited to the purposes peculiar to auctions in their organization of them. They may have many other legitimate purposes – for instance the running of peaceful as well as profitable auctions – and so quite properly exclude from the auction anyone likely to cause an affray, even when such people are wealthy. The conditions of fair discrimination are preserved in this, however. The likelihood that some people will cause trouble is highly relevant to the purpose of keeping the peace.

To believe in equality of opportunity, then, is not to believe that everyone must have an equal chance of success in everything they attempt. Neither is it to believe that only considerations strictly relevant to the various social activities in which individuals engage for mutual benefit can properly be used to discriminate between them. But there are characteristics of people which we can see to be irrelevant to any activity whatever, discrimination on the basis of which is guaranteed to be unfair. A belief in social equality is accordingly at its strongest when it is understood to be a belief in equality of opportunity for everyone regardless of such generally irrelevant characteristics.

The most obvious of these are colour and gender. It seems impossible, except in very special circumstances (an example might be the casting of Othello) to make colour relevant to the conduct of social relations, and though there are more circumstances in which discrimination on grounds of gender is proper (in the allocation of maternity beds, for instance), it also seems true that, in general, gender is irrelevant in the distribution of opportunities. Indeed, almost all of the arguments brought against the idea of sexual equality implicitly concede this point. In the face of the suggestion that men and women ought in general to be treated equally, people very often argue that there are important differences between men and women – that women are weaker, or more emotional and less capable of detachment, or have a lower level of intelligence. But even were we to grant the truth of these claims (and they are certainly *not* true), we should have extracted from the people who make them an admission that it is not being a woman *as such* that is relevant to employment etc., but being weaker or more emotional or less clever. In other words, the mere fact that some individual is a woman *is* irrelevant, so that were we to be considering a woman who was in point of fact as strong, as clever or as stable as most men (and let us just assume for the sake of the argument that in this she is different to the general run of women), there would be no reason not to hire her.

The same point is to be made about arguments for racism. Leaving aside the by now well-established fact that there is no biological basis for the concept of 'race', we may observe that those who believe in racial segregation or racial discrimination usually base their beliefs on claims about the inherent stupidity, idleness, or deviousness of the race they love to hate. But the use of such arguments is itself an admission that it is *not* enough to point to racial origin in order to justify discriminating against people; we must back this up with some further reason, such as their stupidity or idleness, which will indeed be relevant. And once again granting for the sake of argument the patent falsehoods about common racial properties upon which such reasoning relies, by their own argument racists are forced to acknowledge that there would be no reason to discriminate against any clever or hardworking member of the despised race.

What is important, however, is not the feebleness of racist or sexist arguments, but the *general* irrelevance of race and gender in the distribution of opportunities, for it is this which justifies their social proscription. By social proscription here, we need not mean simply that such unfair discrimination should be against the law, but that it may rightly be held to be wrong and that societies, our own and others, may properly be criticized for permitting or sustaining it. What is a more interesting and in many ways more important question, however, is how far society or the state is justified in taking positive steps to remedy social inequalities that have arisen between different groups of people from past discrimination on these irrelevant grounds. This is, in fact, an important question in contemporary social philosophy – the justification of positive discrimination or affirmative action.

Unfair discrimination and affirmative action

We have seen that freedom for the individual to engage fruitfully in social activities depends upon certain conditions being satisfied. These conditions together make up what we are calling 'equality of opportunity', and they include freedom from unfair discrimination, by law if necessary, but more importantly by the established beliefs and practices of a good society. Unfair discrimination is discrimination between different members of the same society which is based upon considerations wholly irrelevant to the activity in question, and though most of the features that make individuals the people they are can be used to make relevant discriminations, the point still holds that, where there are generally irrelevant features, it is improper to discriminate on the basis of them. And there are indeed some such features, colour and gender being two.

If we take together the conclusions of the first three chapters, then, we may summarize the position we have reached by saying that a good society will be one in which individuals are free to pursue and promote their own interests as they see fit, regardless of colour or gender. There is, however, an important qualification to be entered here. In a free society individuals may do as they wish as far as possible. This includes doing what they wish with what is their own. But such freedom seems to carry with it freedom to discriminate on grounds of colour or gender. A man who owns his own house is, in a free society, free to decide who he will sell it to, and if he decides not to sell it to a black person because of the person's colour then, however deplorable this may be from a moral point of view, he must remain free to do so just because real freedom includes the freedom to act immorally. The freedom of individuals to do as they wish with what is their own, then, requires us to allow them freedom simply to choose on grounds of colour or gender (indeed there is good reason to think that sexual freedom just is an ungrounded freedom of choice between others on grounds of gender).

The perception that individuals do indeed have the right in a free society to discriminate on grounds of colour or gender, however objectionable it may be to do so, has sometimes led people to suppose that this outlaws any social policy which tries to counteract social inequality between groups. But this is not so. We must not think of social discrimination simply as individual discrimination multiplied many times, but as something *structural*, that is, built into the functioning of a society. To see the difference, compare the case of the woman who, because she hates black people, will not sell her house to a black person, with that of someone who has no racial prejudice, but knows that selling to a black person will start a decline in house values which will badly affect friends and neighbours. The second case is importantly different because the discrimination arises not from personal choice but from the operation of good reasoning about house values in a society in which there is widespread racial discrimination. To try to alter this sort of inequality is not to attack the freedom of the individual to sell, but to attack the conditions under which the sales available to him or her are restricted. In this way, an attack on racialism can be seen to be the promotion of freedom.

What this implies is that the proponents of a free society, while allowing that individuals must always remain free to indulge themselves in irrational discrimination, can nevertheless advocate the sort of policies designed to combat racism that have become widespread in recent years. This is because the point of what is called, variously, reverse discrimination, positive discrimination, preferential hiring and affirmative action (the term I shall in fact use) is not to undo or redress unfair discrimination by individuals against other individuals, but to promote equality of opportunity for groups of people who *as a group* have suffered systematic unfair discrimination in the past.

Structural inequality

From here on I shall restrict my examples to the position of women and black people because these are the two cases that have prompted the most widely publicized affirmative action programmes. But of course in the real world there are many other groups unfairly discriminated against – Jews in the Soviet Union and Palestinian Arabs in Israel are particularly clear cases, for instance – and the arguments to be considered would apply equally well in all these cases, because in all of them the discrimination is not just a matter of individual conduct but has something *structural* about it – it arises from the way the institutions work in the various societies in which these groups live. And it is this structural discrimination that is important from the point of view of social philosophy and policy, not just because at an individual level the effects of discrimination are less serious, though they probably are, but because it is at a structural level that unfair discrimination is the enemy of freedom.

Some of its ways are very subtle. One of them is social expectation, which often eliminates the need for open discrimination by inducing self-selected exclusion. For instance, in most societies there are very few women surgeons, principally because women are not expected to enter such a highly skilled profession, both by others and by themselves. Indeed, precisely for this reason they may themselves choose unsuitable subjects at school and college so that by the time they come to the age at which surgery is a real option, they are ineligible on highly relevant grounds. But of course the relevant grounds result from the earlier application of irrelevant ones. This is indeed the general nature of structural unfair discrimination; it legitimizes discrimination on grounds of colour or gender by sustaining the very prejudice on which, in its turn, it feeds. This is the point illustrated by the earlier example of selling a house. Though we must agree that certain characteristics like colour and gender are in general irrelevant to the proper conduct of social affairs, paradoxically the belief that they *are* relevant can make them so. There is a sense in which, in a society where racial discrimination is widely practised, the colour of a person's skin becomes highly relevant in deciding whether or not to employ him or her. For example, it might be the case that were a restaurateur to employ a black waiter, the business would suffer drastically because of the prejudices of those who would now refuse to eat there. In such circumstances, the restaurateur has good reason to refuse to employ someone black, and yet in a perfectly obvious sense, being black is irrelevant to being a good or a bad waiter. What is wrong is not the individual restaurateur's behaviour, but the society in which he or she has to conduct business.

The conclusion we should draw from these cases is that remedying unfair discrimination is not merely a matter of ensuring fairness on the part of individuals. It may also require steps to be taken which will attack the problem at a *social* level too, the justification being, as always, the freedom of the individual. And if we add to these considerations about freedom the claim that a prosperous society will be one in which employers have the pick of the best people for each and every occupation, we will begin to see still further reason to seek change in any society in which the aspirations of individuals are restricted on irrelevant grounds, for it both prevents individuals from getting the best out of their lives, and it prevents society as a whole from getting the best out of the individuals who comprise it.

It is precisely this sort of change in society at which affirmative action programmes are aimed and it is in terms of this goal that they are to be judged. But to see the real force of this observation we need first to consider the most serious objections to them.

Objections to affirmative action

Affirmative action is the practice of giving preference to candidates from hitherto unfairly treated groups in the matters of jobs, contracts, college places, scholarships and the like. One objection is that such affirmative action is futile, because by favouring black people or women *now* we are doing nothing to redress or even compensate for the wrongs done to those who have been unfairly discriminated against *in the past*. This point is not obvious to everyone, perhaps because of certain misleading ways of speaking. If, instead of talking about individual black people and women, we talk about 'the black' or 'woman', we may easily fall into the way of supposing that in advancing the interests of one black person or one woman we are advancing the interests of a whole group. But this is patently false. To help more and more black people to become teachers, doctors and lawyers may be a very good thing, but its goodness cannot lie with its being compensation to black people long since dead who failed, as a result of unfair discrimination, to be any of these things, just because they are not there to be compensated. It follows that, if the rationale for affirmative action is supposed to be the redressing of ancient wrongs, it plainly fails.

Those who bring this objection to affirmative action pro- grammes are both right and wrong. They are right in their claim that contemporary positive discrimination can do nothing to undo past negative discrimination and that consequently affirmative action cannot be justified as some species of retributive justice. But they are quite wrong if they suppose that this is an objection to affirmative action as such. Rather it is an objection to one defence of it, and from the destruction of that defence we cannot reasonably conclude that no other defence can be constructed. The objection shows us, however, that any successful defence should be future looking rather than backward looking, which is to say that the defence of affirmative action must lie with what the society of the future *will* be like, not what the society of the past *was* like.

But there are at least two further objections to affirmative action which turn upon the suggestion that, whatever it may do for future societies, affirmative action is wrong in itself. The first of these is perhaps the commonest objection of all, namely that affirmative action programmes involve a radical inconsistency since they practise discrimination on grounds of colour or gender supposedly on the grounds that such discrimination is unfair. But if it is unfair to discriminate *against* a candidate on grounds of the candidate's colour, it is surely just as unfair to discriminate in favour. Race and gender do not become any more relevant because discrimination based on them works in the opposite direction.

But this contradiction is more apparent than real. We saw a little earlier, in the example of the restaurateur, that though in general colour is irrelevant to the proper conduct of social intercourse, contingent circumstances can make it relevant. The restaurateur may well regret the fact that he or she cannot employ a black person, but in refusing to do so he or she is guided solely by highly relevant business considerations, and for this reason no blame attaches to him or her. The fault lies with the society within which the restaurateur must operate. What this means is that, regrettably, it *is* possible to have good reason to discriminate on grounds of colour – in a racist society a prospective employer has little choice. But it is a point of which proponents of affirmative action programmes may also avail themselves to good effect, for they, too, have good reason to discriminate on grounds of colour, only in their case the reason arises not from the unfortunate workings of racial prejudice, but from the desire and intention to bring an end to that prejudice. Their positive discrimination is justified precisely because it is aimed at reducing negative discrimination. There is therefore no contradiction, any more than there is a contradiction in the behaviour of the gardener who nips some rose buds in order to make others grow larger.

Of course, good intentions are not enough. Just as the mere *possibility* (as opposed to a real likelihood) of customers staying away would be an insufficient justification for the restaurateur's refusal to hire a black person, so actions taken merely in the name of reverse discrimination are not enough. They must be such as actually to make a difference. It is morally important that affirmative action programmes be effective. This is an important point to which we shall return, but before doing so we should consider the third objection to affirmative action programmes. Like the second, this objection holds that, whether or not they do any good, there is a principled objection to them.

This third objection turns on the idea that in rejecting the best candidate for some position on grounds of colour or gender we are violating his or her right to the job. In the United States at present there is some reason to think, with respect to certain job opportunities, that a talented white heterosexual male with no physical handicaps may be seriously disadvantaged. This situation has come about through the aggressive promotion of affirmative action programmes. But there can be no reason to think that such people are not often the best candidates, precisely because, if the presuppositions of the affirmative action programme itself are true, white middle-class males will have had the highest educational opportunities and as a group are therefore more likely to produce top-rate candidates. What we should conclude from this, according to this third objection, is that across the United States the wrong people are getting the jobs.

Some people have responded to this sort of complaint by modifying the scope of their affirmative action and claiming that preference according to colour or gender is permissible only where there are two equally well-qualified candidates. The response meets the objection, because if the candidates are equally well qualified, the person who gets the post, though not uniquely well qualified, will be as good as any other available candidate, and consequently cannot be said to be the wrong candidate. But in fact the response makes more of a concession than it needs to, since the objection fails to stick even where less well-qualified candidates are appointed.

This is because the objection makes two false assumptions. First it assumes that the best candidate has a right to the job. This is not true. If I offer you a job I am offering you a benefit to which you have no prior entitlement. The fact that I decide to offer it to you creates an entitlement on your part only in so far as the offer constitutes some sort of promise or contract, which I then have an obligation to keep. But any qualifications you have function in this only as reasons which help me decide to whom I should offer the job. They do not determine whose job it is by right.

But besides this there is a second and more important assumption at work here, the assumption that we know, independently of colour or gender, who the best qualified candidate is, that colour and gender cannot be appropriate qualifications. But we saw earlier that they can. The blackness of the waiter was, in a certain context, a *dis*qualification, and in a different context it might thus be a qualification. Similarly, though a black candidate for a job as teacher might have less good certificates or less experience than a white candidate, the likely attitudes of black children to a white teacher (hostile *or* subservient) may easily make his or her blackness a more telling qualification. Likewise, *if* it is the case that the appointment of black people and women will serve to break down prejudice and make for a freer and more prosperous society in the future, then their blackness and womanliness *are* qualifications.

Affirmative action and effectiveness

There is reason, then, to reject the objections to affirmative action. It is very important to observe, however, that the rational rejection of these objections depends at crucial points on the effectiveness of such programmes. This is because preferential hiring according to race and gender is to be defended only as a temporary practice designed to eliminate the sort of society in which it is needed. But for this defence to work it has to be the case that this is indeed the aim and end of affirmative action.

The first point to make, perhaps, is that, human nature being what it is, this is often not the motivation of those who engage in affirmative action. Not infrequently it is, on the contrary, a rather unsavoury mixture of guilt on the part of men and white people and a desire for revenge on the part of black people and women. Such motivation, however, shares the defects of the appeal to past injustices; contemporary white men who have not made a practice of discrimination have no reason to feel guilty on the part of those who have done so in the past, and contemporary black women cannot avenge themselves on white racist men whose deeds are in the past.

But more important is the point that even if affirmative action programmes are undertaken with the best of motives, always assuming discrimination on grounds of colour or gender to be unfair, they are justified only in so far as they stand a good chance of making some difference. And the knowledge that they really do depends, not upon moral or philosophical argument, but upon careful empirical studies within the society in question. This is an important conclusion to reach. It means that the effectiveness of affirmative action programmes must come under continuous scrutiny if they are to be justified, because it is only by judging their effectiveness that we can decide whether they are or not.

The matter of their effectiveness has two aspects. On the one hand we must be able to see that affirmative action is actually altering popular prejudice and other structural causes of unfair discrimination; and on the other, assuming it does make a difference, we must be ready to detect the point at which a tolerable equilibrium between races or sexes is established, because, since it is at this point it will cease to be justifiable, it is at this point that affirmative action must be phased out. Social monitoring of this kind, as we shall see in chapter 8, is itself a difficult business. The point to stress, however, is that from every point of view it must be undertaken. Obviously this is true of those who suffer the effects of structural inequality, since they are unlikely to be satisfied with high-sounding policies that accomplish little or nothing. But it is just as true from the point of view of those who initiate them. If the justification of affirmative action lies in the changes it brings about, the moral

5

Health Care Provision

The argument up to this point has led us to the view that every political action and social policy should be judged good or bad in so far as it advances the interests of individuals. Most important of these interests is in fact the freedom to decide for oneself what those interests are and how, when and whether they should be promoted. To agree that this is so is effectively to agree that the good society is a free society.

Some social theorists have thought that such freedom is possible only at the expense of social equality and social justice. Others have argued that in a truly free society social justice will take care of itself. But we have seen, in the consideration first of social justice and then of affirmative action programmes, that neither of these claims is true. The sort of equality that is often called social justice is not, despite the name, an alternative or competing social goal to individual freedom, but something whose value resides precisely in the contribution it makes to individual freedom. This carries the further implication that the strongest defence of the sorts of social policy which are usually called egalitarian will construe them as a means of promoting and protecting individual freedom.

On the other hand, we have also seen that real freedom for the individual in society does not necessarily come about by itself, but may be limited by peculiarly social constraints. Real freedom may need, as a precondition of its existence, many of those social measures traditionally favoured by egalitarians. In fact this is, we have seen, an effective explanation and defence of affirmative action programmes. A similar line of thought has often been developed with respect to medical care. Many illnesses are incapacitating in one way or another, so that it is initially quite plausible to argue that society, in providing its citizens with a health system, is engaged not just in curing illnesses and promoting health, but also in promoting individual freedom. It is to this argument that we now turn, and to the topic of health care in general.

To make good the argument that the social provision of health care facilities is one of those background conditions without which the freedom of individuals to live their own lives as they think best is impossible or at least seriously impaired, we have to think first about health and what it is. No one doubts that health is something valuable. This is what makes the very word itself a plus word, one which carries automatic commendation, and what makes its opposite, sickness, a negative one. To appeal on behalf of the sick is immediately to be recognized as someone engaged in good work. Yet this attitude to health, once we begin to think about it, is far too general, because it calls up images that are in point of fact quite inappropriate to many of the sorts of case with which the promotion of health must be concerned.

When we think of the sick, those in need of doctors, we very easily and naturally picture frail and pain-racked bodies lying passively between crisp white sheets. But at the same time we know perfectly well that many more, probably a large majority, of the people who use medical services have much less romantic ailments – like acne, constipation and ingrowing toenails. Further, we have a picture of illness as something *fateful* – something that strikes people without reason or regard to merit and is a part of the 'natural lottery' mentioned before. But again this is true of only a very limited number of cases. Throughout the world, far more headaches are caused by hangovers than by brain aneurisms, and, certainly in Western countries and the Soviet bloc, excessive eating is the cause of many more medical problems than hunger or anatomical deficiencies. Even very serious illnesses – lung cancer, cirrhosis of the liver, AIDS – which do threaten patients with a slow and painful death may in many cases be directly traceable to a self-chosen life style.

This is not to say that these ailments warrant neither

sympathy nor assistance. On the contrary, all of them call for help and treatment. The alleviation of pain and suffering, whatever their cause, is always to be valued. But what it does mean is that we cannot regard 'health' in a single light and hence cannot suppose at the outset that its promotion within society, by the state or in any other way, is to be treated as a unitary subject. This means that what may reasonably be said about, for instance, the prevention of rickets in children may not carry any implications for what is to be said about the prevention of knee injuries among joggers or lung diseases among smokers. In short, the concepts of 'health' and 'ill health' do not refer to just one thing and its opposite, but to a cluster of different conditions in which organisms may find themselves. Consequently, the rationale of the provision of health facilities is not likely to consist in a single formula either.

Health and autonomy

These initial reflections on the concept of health suggest that the prospects are not bright for theories which offer a single explanation and justification of the place of health care in society. People have sometimes supposed, for instance, that the social provision of doctors and hospitals is to be explained and justified by appeal to the following line of thought. Pain and suffering are incapacitating. They prevent us from pursuing our lives fully as autonomous agents and create an unfair inequality between the sick and the healthy. Consequently, in a good society the services of doctors and hospitals, whose business is with the alleviation of pain and suffering, will be made freely available to all, regardless of their ability to pay, as one way of promoting the freedom and equality of individuals.

Now typically, perhaps, doctors and hospitals *are* thought to have the alleviation of pain and suffering as their central concern. This conception of doctoring is questionable, but even if we think it true, we must also acknowledge that pain is not necessarily debilitating. Often it is merely disagreeable. In fact the effective control of most pains is relatively new in the accomplishments of medical science, and hence in the experience of humanity, so that at most times and places, human beings have had to and have been able to control their affairs and conduct their lives despite the pain they had to suffer. Indeed there are many celebrated examples of individuals who reached the height of their powers despite constant pain, suffering and handicap, sometimes perhaps because of it – Beethoven is one very notable case – so that it would be odd indeed to think the absence of pain and suffering as such a necessary condition of a fruitful and self-realizing existence.

Moreover, even in our own day pain itself is not always and everywhere thought of as a sufficient ground for medical assistance. Strenuous physical exercise causes pain, but the pain that it causes is regarded as healthy. Breathlessness, when it results from running races, though it may not differ much at a physiological level, is rightly regarded quite differently from the breathlessness that results from emphysema or bronchitis. Indeed, in some rare cases, pain is actually welcomed by those who undergo it – in initiation ceremonies, for instance – and in many of these the whole point of the ceremony turns on the belief that an ability to undergo pain without recourse to methods of alleviation is a mark of attaining autonomy or adulthood.

But even if we could plausibly argue that pain impairs autonomy, we should not have arrived at an explanation of the need for health care, because doctors and hospitals are almost as widely used for the correction and treatment of non-painful conditions, for births and birth control, plastic surgery, mental disorders, drug dependency, weight control, giving blood, and the promotion of nutrition. The alleviation of pain may be their main business, but it is certainly not their only one.

What both these considerations show is that the argument as set out has at least two important errors in it. First, it is not true that a health service is solely (perhaps not even principally) concerned with alleviating pain, and secondly, even if it were, this would not imply that it was an important instrument for promoting autonomy. Neither consideration is meant to suggest, however, that these other uses of medical services are improper, or should have only secondary importance in hospitals and surgeries. What it is meant to show is that, just as the concept of health covers a wide range of conditions, so the concept of a health service must be understood to imply a wide range of services, and because this is so, we cannot explain or justify its place in society in the simple way suggested.

Health as a value

But there is another, even more important implication to be drawn from these items of common knowledge. 'Health' is itself an evaluative term, and if that is so, questions about what provision should be made for it will be more intimately connected with the autonomy of the individual than any 'background condition' theory could make them.

To see the full force of this point, we might usefully consider first a related concept, namely that of fitness. Now people do speak of 'fitness' as though it were one thing, and refer to themselves and others as 'fit' and 'unfit'. But over two thousand years ago the ancient Greek philosopher Aristotle pointed out that fitness is not a physiological condition which people either meet up to or not, like being six feet tall, but a *relative* term. What is fitness in one person might not be fitness in another. It does not take much reflection to see that the question 'Are you fit?' invites the further question 'Fit for what?'. To be 'fit' as the world generally understands the term is to be roughly the right sort of weight for your height and to able to take part in reasonably strenuous physical activity without collapsing breathless in no time at all. But it ought to be obvious to anyone that the fittest office worker is quite unfit for the Olympic Games, and the most persistent jogger is unfit for commando survival courses. To insist that any given individual is 'fit' or 'unfit' in an absolute sense, that is, to treat being fit as though it were like being six feet tall, is to make the mistake of assuming that fitness for one activity (jogging, usually) is fitness for all. The truth is that, despite common usage, fitness is always relative to some task or activity, and there is no such thing as fitness itself.

The importance of seeing this lies in the accompanying perception that fitness is properly an evaluative term. We assess someone's fitness *for* something. But this has the further implication that, again despite common speech, we cannot

meaningfully commend 'fitness' as such. We can only commend something as making you fit for some activity or other.
This means that the desirability of being fit in that particular
way depends upon the desirability of the activity in question.
You only have reason to fit yourself for a task if you have
reason to perform that task. 'You ought not to be so unfit'
invites the question 'Unfit for what?'. If the answer is 'Unfit to
jog four miles a day', we must now ask, 'Why ought I to jog
four miles a day?'. The answer, 'In order to get fit', is obviously
circular, and for this reason quite insufficient. What we need is
an answer that will explain the desirability of jogging, and
people whose fitness is criticized in this way will have to satisfy
themselves of the value of jogging before any of the criticism
sticks. If, as a matter of fact, there is no value to being able to jog
long distances, there will be no disvalue in being unfit to do it.
(The claim that the value of jogging lies in preventing heart
attacks in later life is the right *sort* of answer, though it may in fact
be false.)

If fitness is a relative term, and hence an evaluative one, so
too is health. This may seem initially a very implausible claim,
because health, we might think, is not valuable *for* anything, but
valuable in itself. And this is true. But the relativity arises in
what counts as health. We saw a little earlier that 'health' is a
concept that covers a wide range of different phenomena. It is
not easy to say what links all these together, but one likely
suggestion is that they refer to different ways in which the body
may function which are thought desirable and undesirable.
Now the important point to grasp is that the desirability and
undesirability of these different ways does not arise from their
physiological nature, but from the aims and ends of individuals.
Certain painful ailments – heart disease, stomach ulcers,
eczema, psoriasis – count as ill health and in need of treatment,
others, though no less physiologically based – aching muscles
after rugby, labour pains, the sting of pierced ears, hangovers –
do not. No doubt part of the difference is in their relative
seriousness, but the important point to focus on here is that
what counts as health and ill health is not just a matter of
anatomical pain or physiological condition, but of how these
are assessed and understood.

Sometimes this means how they are assessed and understood
by society in general, and sometimes it means how they are

assessed and understood by the individual who undergoes them. It is the second case that is most important here. If what counts as 'health' and 'ill health' is at least in some instances a question which turns on the evaluations of individuals, this implies at once that those who believe in autonomy will not want to see the freedom of individuals to decide these things for themselves pre-empted by a social institution which determines in advance, through the provision of facilities, what is and is not a matter of health. An example will make this point clearer. Are you ill if you are growing short-sighted as you get older? Most people would say 'no', not because they do not know that short-sightedness is a malfunctioning of the eyes (myopia is the technical term and makes it sound more 'medical'), but because they regard it as part of the process of aging rather than ill health, and they continue to regard it as such even where it is seriously disabling, as in the case of airline pilots.

The point this sort of case illustrates is that we cannot consider 'health' to be a purely physiological notion, one which could, in principle at any rate, be given a clinical definition. What is and is not ill health is determined not just by physiology or anatomy, but by what does and does not matter to people and how it matters. To see this is to see that evaluation is built into the notion of health. But if that is so, health is only one value amongst others, and this, as we shall see, is a conclusion of considerable consequence.

Health and other values

What we think of as ill health, then, is in part determined by what we *care about*. But ill health is not all we care about nor health all that we seek, and faced with a choice between health and the other things we value, we are not logically obliged or psychologically predisposed to put health first. This is not something that is immediately obvious to everyone. The claim, when true, that 'You are ruining your health' is sometimes thought to be a knock-down argument against whatever it is you are doing. But it is no such thing, because there is nothing unintelligible about preferring other goods to health. Another instance of the same mistake informs a great deal of so-called health education, which very often rests upon the false assumption that you have only to convince people that, for example, 'Smoking will damage their health' in order to stop them smoking. When, after a time, it is evident that they are not stopping, the 'education' campaign is usually said to have failed. But it may well have succeeded. There is nothing puzzling about having made people aware of the likely effects of smoking cigarettes and finding them decide that the pleasure of smoking is still worth the risk. It is precisely the same sort of reasoning that leads people to choose a night on the town in the sure and certain knowledge that they will feel wretched next morning.

Both these examples illustrate the competition between the value of health and the value of pleasure, but health competes with other values too. Some of these conflicts are in fact very common features of human existence. We are thoroughly familiar with occasional preferences for beauty and fashion over health – failure to wear a hearing aid, persistence with shoes that cause blisters on the heel – and there are lots of clashes between the pursuit of health and the value of sport – the love of motor racing, skiing, boxing and jogging often overrides the desire to avoid the sorts of physical injury which these pastimes very frequently cause.

Now it is an important part of the freedom of individuals to be able to make choices of precisely this kind, and this means that it is an important part of individual freedom to able to decide when one's health should take priority over other goals and values and when it should not. But such a judgement enters practical decision-making about long-term provision for health as much as it does short-term choices between different actions or activities. Faced with a headache that requires an aspirin and with the desire for an ice-cream, but with insufficient money to deal with both, the right to decide whether to buy aspirin or ice cream lies with the individual whose headache and whose desire it is. But equally, faced with a choice between health insurance and a better house, the right to make that choice also seems to lie with the individual whose health and housing are at stake.

FREEDOM OF CHOICE IN HEALTH CARE

This conclusion carries important implications for social policy. If it really is the case that the choice between health insurance and other goods, being a choice between different values, is properly a matter for the individual whose well-being is affected, there can be no justification for a society-wide health service which provides uniform health care, funded out of compulsory health insurance. There can be no justification for such a system because under it decisions about the relative importance of health over other goods, and about the proportion of resources that should be devoted to health rather than other things, are taken out of the hands of the individual and made by some central authority. If by right, however, such decisions properly belong to those individuals, their being usurped in this way is plainly indefensible.

As a result, it seems a free society cannot be one in which a compulsory society-wide health system operates, because, it will be recalled, a free society is one in which individuals as far as possible make for themselves those decisions which affect their own interests. Clearly, my state of health is something that is in my interest, and hence the degree to which and the way in which it ought to be promoted are things for me to decide.

The argument that has brought us to this point (which I shall call 'the freedom argument') is a fairly simple one, yet very many countries in the world have health systems which the conclusion of the argument shows to be indefensible. How can this be? Surely there must be powerful arguments on the other side?

The fact that, upon reflection, some conclusion is clearly correct does not always make it obvious to everyone. There are indeed arguments which many have found persuasive and which suggest the desirability of national health services. I shall argue that these arguments are in fact flawed and that the initial conclusion which we have arrived at with comparative ease is correct. But to do so convincingly it is necessary to give serious and sympathetic consideration to these other arguments, especially since many people have often been impressed by them.

Arguments against freedom of choice

The freedom argument we have just considered rests upon a number of important contentions which many writers have been quick to dispute. Four of these are especially important. First, it relies heavily on the claim that in common speech the term 'health care' covers a wide variety of different things and hence cannot be justified in just one way. Secondly, it supposes that because health may be valued differently by different individuals it is a matter about which the individual alone must decide. Thirdly, it assumes that the freedom of the individual in decisions over his or her own health cannot be realized in a compulsory state-run health system. Fourthly, it makes the freedom of choice for the individual overridingly important. All four of these claims are disputable.

Consider first the claim that 'health care' means different things, not all of which have to do with sickness, pain or injury. It may be true that in everyday life we think of a variety of different things as being the responsibility of doctors, some of which really have very little to do with health in a narrower sense (contraception is as good an example as any). But usually these are very much the minority. The vast majority of problems that doctors are asked to deal with really do have to do with injuries and diseases which have the common feature of causing suffering and/or threatening disability and death. Moreover, even if it is true that 'health' and 'ill health' as commonly used do not always refer to pain, disease and injury, we are still at liberty to restrict the claims for a national health service to serious cases of illness and injury. And if we do, it is pretty evident that the first step of the freedom argument accomplishes nothing. To advocate the establishment (or defence) of a national health service, where we understand 'health' to refer not to all the things that doctors commonly do but to the treatment of serious illness and injury, is to advocate a distinctive type of service, and hence one which may indeed make possible a uniform justification.

The second point of the freedom argument for individual freedom in medical care – that health may be valued differently by different individuals – can be dealt with, it appears, no less speedily. Once more, the claim is, in general, true only in a limited number and range of cases. Hardly anyone prefers fun to paralysis or looking good to having a heart attack. While it may be true in theory that people *could* choose differently, in fact the vast majority of people make the same choice and give priority to health.

To undermine the third element in the argument – the assumption that freedom of choice for the individual cannot be institutionalized in a compulsory state service – we have to see that individuals may set about securing their own interests in different ways. In societies where individuals are left to look after their own health, we know as a matter of recorded fact that there is a great deal of suffering and ill health as a result. Part of the cause of this, perhaps the largest part, is to be found in the foolish and imprudent choices individuals make, for many of these choices, though ill considered, have long-term consequences both for the individuals and their families. Now a firm belief in the right of the individual to choose is often thought to bring with it the obligation to accept this suffering as the price of freedom, but in fact there is nothing in the argument which says that individuals themselves cannot temper their support for individual liberty with concern for individual welfare, just because they recognize the likely effects of unrestricted freedom. Why must we, or they, take the view that the individual has to pay the price of his or her mistakes for ever?

But this possibility has important consequences. Knowing that left to their own devices they may make silly choices about health care, and desirous of not being made to pay for these mistakes for ever, individuals may elect to establish a compulsory state system of health care, which will to some extent protect them from themselves. In other words, they will freely call into existence a system which severely constrains their freedom of choice in particular cases, and surely the true champion of freedom must accept their right to do so.

That objection is a powerful one because it assumes the over-riding importance of the individual's right to choose, and thus calls the freedom argument into question by trading on one of its own assumptions. But an even more profound attack on the argument calls this assumption into question on the grounds that it can only be sustained if we picture individuals as isolated and exclusively self-concerned. But in reality, of course, 'no man is an island, entire of itself'. Those who make decisions about health insurance have children and elderly relatives very often, and if they choose to spend the money on drink instead, others besides them are left at the mercy of illness and injury. Accordingly we could restrict the freedom of the individual on the ground of preventing harm to others.

But it is not just a concern with the general welfare that stands in opposition to a free-for-all in health care. The belief that these other people should not be seriously disadvantaged by the free choice of those who happen to have charge of them marks a concern with *justice*, and balancing the interests of conflicting parties. There is nothing in the freedom argument which says we must prefer individual freedom to justice for others.

If these objections are sound, the argument for total individual freedom of choice in health care has failed to establish its case.

This is a conclusion with wider implications. If it is correct, the general doctrine of social individualism as explained and defended in chapters 2 and 3 loses much of its interest, since it has far fewer implications for social policy than may have seemed likely at first. This is because arguments for and against state health schemes are so often thought to be arguments for and against individualism. But the counter-arguments considered here are just as individualist as the position they attack. They make no appeal to the values of community and comradeship, which communitarians might regard a national health system freely available to all as expressing, and this means that the dispute about what sort of health care system we ought to have is not necessarily a dispute between individualist and communitarian values at all. Of course, once we examine the counter-arguments more carefully, it may turn out that this is not the case, but adding the possibility of individualist arguments for socialized medicine to the individualist arguments for affirmative action action in the last chapter, the practical relevance and importance of the arguments in chapters 2 and 3 appears to be diminishing rapidly.

It follows that the examination of the counter-arguments set out in this section are of special interest. We shall discover, I think, that they do rest upon a misperception of the true implications of individualism, but to see this clearly we must now examine them one by one.

Examination of objections to freedom of choice

The idea that there is a 'core' concept of health (and hence of health care), which exclusively picks out the absence or alleviation of pain and sickness and the prevention of death and injury, is hard to overcome. It is the absence of any such core concept which led to the orginal suggestion that the justification of health care provision is unlikely to take just one form. Nevertheless, it must be admitted, as the first objection maintains, that we *could* use the terms 'health' and 'health care' in a restricted way, to cover only these specially important cases. But even if we do, we are no nearer a uniform justification of compulsory socialized medicine, because within this restricted concept there is still sufficient variety to generate the same problem as before. Is the sort of reasoning which we could bring in favour of free state help for the sick children of poor parents likely also to support free state help for the hangovers of the rich? Yet the alleviation of pain and sickness and the prevention of injury are no less involved in the assistance of drunks after a party than they are in the care of children in hospital. Certainly, there are important differences between the two cases, but the main point is that they both fall under the concept of health care, even if we restrict that concept to its central and most appealing elements.

But even if we could find a core concept such that everything which fell under it had the same moral 'pull' as does preventing the spread of plague and helping its victims, we still would not have an argument for compulsory socialized medicine, because while it is true, as the second objection alleges, that most people most of the time give priority to life and health over other values, this is not to the point, because the freedom argument is concerned with protecting the right of individual citizens to make their own choices, and this means protecting them from majority opinion as much as from the actions of governments.

It is enough, therefore, to show that evaluations different from those of the majority are *intelligible*; we do not have to show that they are or would be widely accepted.

This is the point at issue in Brian Clark's play *Whose life is it anyway?*. A sculptor has a serious car accident, and despite multiple injuries is brought back to a viable existence by the skilful use of advanced medical technology. He is, nevertheless, quadraplegic, and being deprived of all the things that had previously made life valuable – chiefly sculpting, dancing, and sex – he decides to refuse the treatment which will keep him alive. All of those who have to deal with him disagree with his decision and refuse to comply with it. The principal doctor, in fact, overrules it and forcibly gives him medication. Eventually the sculptor persuades an attorney to take the case to law, at which point there is an attempt on the part of the doctors to have him certified as unfit to make proper decisions because of clinical depression. The case turns on whether or not he is clinically depressed, but the hearing firmly establishes that his decision to refuse treatment at the cost of his own life is a rational exercise of evaluation, and the doctors are ordered to desist in their efforts to preserve him.

Two points of general relevance to the topic of this section are illustrated by this play. First, we have to accept that even the decision to reject life itself can be a rationally considered one, and must therefore be respected even if we think it wrong (as most of the other characters in the play do). Secondly, just who ought to be making the decision is crucially important. It is Harrison (the sculptor) not Emerson (the doctor) who has a right to make the decision, for the very simple reason that it is Harrison's not Emerson's life that is at stake. What the play illustrates is that even where the direst consequence – death – is at stake, it can still be wrong to remove evaluative choices from those who alone have a right to make them. So, the fact that most people, perhaps the vast majority, would prefer life, even as a quadraplegic, to death, does not show that anyone can justifiably be forced to make the same evaluation.

The truth of this has wider application. If I cannot justifiably be compelled to value my life more than my death, or my health more than my pleasure, I cannot justifiably be compelled to make provision for one at the expense of the other. This conclusion holds good no matter how uniformly serious the things are which we bring under the concepts of health and health care, which is why the objection to the freedom argument must be rejected, even if the first were to stand.

This brings us to the third objection. Those who object to compulsory systems of socialized medicine do so because they think them opposed to individual freedom of choice. But why should people in society, aware that they will be tempted not to make proper provision for times of sickness, not freely choose to introduce a system which will compulsorily protect them from their own imprudence? The answer is that there is no reason why they should not do this. But there is a reason why *other people* should not do this for them, namely that they have no right to. And, under the familiar state-run national systems of health care financed out of taxation, this is precisely what is happening. It is not that healthy individuals compel themselves to make provision for times of sickness, but that the state compels them.

People sometimes think that in a democracy this is not so, because through democratic institutions individuals have the opportunity to express their support for or dissent from different social policies. But even if it is true that democracy provides an important vehicle for the expression of dissent from majority opinion, it does not follow that minorities have power over their own affairs. Someone who believes passionately in private health care, for instance, may have the freedom to campaign and vote for the abolition of a compulsory system, but not have the freedom, should the vote be lost, to withdraw from it. His or her freedom of expression, therefore, does not in any way lessen the coercive nature of the system. Laws arrived at democratically are still laws, and unjust laws arrived at democratically are still unjust.

Certainly it is evident that individuals often do have good reason to make promises and contracts which will secure benefits in the future at some considerable cost now. This is true of an insurance policy. I pay now and for some time, at the expense of present interests, in anticipation of greater future benefit. And knowing, perhaps, that in the middle years of my life I will be tempted to cash in my policy, I might sign a contract making this legally impossible. In this way I now bind myself to do things which, in the not too distant future, I may not want to do. But for such schemes to be compatible with the fundamental rights and freedoms of the individual, they must be freely entered into. This marks the essential difference between legally enforceable health insurance agreements and state-run schemes of socialized medicine financed out of taxation: the former but not the latter are voluntarily entered into, even in a democracy.

The freedom of the individual is indeed freedom to do more than make choices between current options, and this is the truth that is to be found in the third objection to the freedom argument. But it does not provide any grounds upon which to support a compulsory state system of health care provision.

The fourth and final objection to the freedom argument pointed to its obsessive concern with the individual whose health is at issue. But others may be adversely affected by health care decisions as well as the person whose health it is. For this reason justice is at issue as much as liberty.

There are two sorts of effect that are usually brought into the discussion here. First, the ill health of one individual may adversely affect family and friends. Secondly, the cost of modern medical technology means that the refusal of some to contribute to a mutually advantageous health care system can deprive others of any system at all. A national health care system to which all are obliged to contribute, and upon whose assistance everyone may call freely, ensures that irresponsible individuals who do not care about their own health do not thereby injure the health and welfare of others.

This is an important argument because any free society must accept the principle that the individual can only have such liberties as are compatible with the same liberties for everyone. Consequently, if my freedom to choose to be ill prevents you from exercising your freedom to be healthy, there is reason to restrict it. And we can think of clear cases of this – the compulsory treatment of those with contagious diseases, for instance. But we must nevertheless be careful how we use this argument. There are two important points at which a free society must stick. First, individuals cannot justifiably be obliged to value health more than other goods, and secondly, the fact that there will be an advantage to others is not in itself sufficient to justify coercive action against the individual. These are points that will be discussed at greater length in the next chapter, but here it should be enough to observe that any system which compels me to forego expenditure on housing in favour of expenditure on health, as a tax-supported system of health care does, violates the first of these principles, and the fact that others benefit from my being forced to contribute is not sufficient, by itself, to justify that coercion. The price of many goods might be reduced and hence their purchasers benefitted if more people were forced to buy them. But no one thinks that this would justify compulsory purchase (though something like this line of thought is at work in farm subsidy systems).

The fourth objection, then, is no more a refutation of the freedom argument than any of the first three. What it does, at best, is draw attention to the need for a free society not merely to protect the freedom of the individual, but on occasions to protect its members *from* the freedom of the individual too. In the case of medical provision, this is likely to be specially important for those who are in the care of others, notably children. Whilst it may be true that I ought to be free, if I wish, to ruin my own health, it is not true that I should be permitted to do so at the cost of my children's health, and for this reason the freedom argument must accommodate the protection of children and other vulnerable groups.

In fact, this is just one aspect of another important topic – the place of children in society – and its discussion will therefore be deferred to a chapter of its own.

Summary

We have seen that there is no single uniform concept of health, and that the services on offer from doctors and hospitals may have quite different uses and values. Moreover, even if we think of health, and hence health care, in a narrow sense of alleviating pain and sickness and preventing death and injury, there is still plenty of scope for intelligible disagreement about the import-ance of health in relation to other values. From this it follows that health, and provision for health care, is something which individuals must be left free to decide for themselves, and from this it further follows that there is no justification in a free society for compulsory systems of health care financed out of taxation. Nor does the fact that individuals may freely undertake contracts and obligations whose purpose is to secure future rather than present benefits, or the fact that the interests of others may be bound up with the health of the individual, give us reason to reject this conclusion. At best they show that the fundamental freedom of the individual in matters of health care may require to be set around by certain conditions and constraints.

Health systems and health insurance

People who cling with affection to systems of socialized medicine in the face of the arguments we have been considering often do so because they think the freedom argument to be one that makes them allies of the wrong side in a clash of interests between rich and poor. Whether or not we have socialized medicine, the rich are likely to have access to the best that modern medicine can offer. But in many places, it is widely believed, the introduction of a compulsory public scheme would greatly improve the health of the poor (at the expense of the rich), and in others its abolition would do great damage. And for this reason the freedom argument, however cogent it may appear, often fails to convince. What it needs is a more positively humane image, and this it can, in fact, be given.

Just as a picture of the ravages of a wasting disease distorts our understanding of what sorts of service hospitals generally offer, so another picture dominates our understanding of financing health services. We very easily think of redistribution within a health care system as being the transfer of money from the wealthy, who would otherwise spend it on champagne and caviare, to the poor, who will at last have the money for life-saving medicine. But at the same time we know this picture to be quite false, not just because the wealthy do not always like champagne, but because complicated tax and health insurance schemes are involved whose workings bear little resemblance to the good deeds of Robin Hood. The real choice, then, is between a system under which each individual has his or her chosen form of health insurance, and one in which all are compelled to have the same form.

In the first, ideally, the amount to be paid would be determined by the cover which individuals chose to have, multiplied by the likelihood that persons in that class would need the relevant treatment. So, for instance, women who were insured for emergency heart treatment would pay less than men, homosexual male couples would not contribute to the cost of maternity and gynaecological services, and those who chose not to be kept on life-support machines, should the need for them ever arise, would pay less than those who did. In other words, health insurance would be much like any other form of insurance. In insuring household property we pay according to the scale of the risk and the amount of cover.

The alternative is a health system financed entirely out of taxation, under which individuals are covered against every eventuality they may need, and payment is made according to ability to pay. Thus no matter how poor you are, and no matter how ill, you will always get the treatment you need.

The first system is that which is most obviously compatible with the freedom argument, the second that which appeals to Those who think the interests of the poor should take precedence over the freedom of the rich. But upon examination, I think, we shall discover that this is a misperception. The second system, though it may indeed protect the destitute in a way that the first does not, actually does so at the expense of the poor. To see this we need to look more closely at the nature of taxation and its cost to the individual.

Marginal utility and relative cost

Consider an imaginary health system financed out of taxation which serves 1000 people and costs £1m a year to run. The average contribution per person is £1000, but if contributions are made on the basis of relative income people will actually pay different amounts. It will also be true that people will receive different levels of benefit from it – in any given year some will receive many times the value of their contribution in the form of medical treatment, and others will receive nothing at all.

Take the case of a rich man who, under the scheme, pays a larger sum than anyone else, say £100,000. He falls ill, however, and has very expensive surgery, including a liver transplant necessitated by a lifetime's drunkenness, and prolonged convalescent treatment under a detoxification programme. In all he receives somewhere in the region of £150,000 worth of medical treatment in the course of the year. On the other hand, the 500 poorest contributors to the scheme are healthy. They receive no benefits in the form of medical treatment, and so their contributions of £100 a year are available to subsidize the treatment of the rich drunkard.

It seems highly implausible to defend such a system on the grounds that it serves the interests of the poor, and the implausibility is increased when we consider the real cost involved, that is to say, the cost relative to the individuals concerned.

Here we need to employ the concept of marginal utility, a concept that economists use a good deal. The idea of marginal utility is really very simple: the more of a good you have, the less valuable still more of it will be to you, and the less of a good you have, the greater will be the loss of any of it. For example, if I am the owner of twenty-five cars, the gift of another one is worth far less to me than the gift of the same car would be to someone who has no car at all, since the number of things I can now do that I could not do before is very small, whereas the other person's opportunities are greatly increased. Conversely, if one of my twenty-five cars is taken away, the loss is small compared to that of someone whose only car is taken away.

When it comes to values expressible in figures, marginal utility may be represented on a graduated scale. A pay rise of £15 is worth far more to someone whose weekly income is £60 than it is to someone whose weekly income is worth £600, and worth even less to someone whose weekly income is £6000. Nor is the relationship simply proportional. Someone at this level of income might need more than £3000 a week extra in order to derive the same increase in benefit.

When we return to consider the finances of compulsory health systems which rely upon taxation, we can see that, despite our best efforts to make the taxation system progressive, the real cost to the poor contributor might still be higher than that to the richest. In our example, we need only suppose that the wealthiest individual is enormously wealthy and the poorest quite poor, and the concept of marginal utility will tell us that a charge of £100 actually imposes a greater burden on the poor than £50,000 would on the rich.

In its turn, this means that the care of the indigent, those who cannot pay anything at all, may well fall more heavily on the poor than on the rich, even though the figures suggest otherwise. If £100,000 is needed each year to cover the expenses of the indigent, and is raised by charging one person £50,000 and 500 others £100, this may still mean that the relative cost to the poor in terms of benefits foregone is higher.

Under a system of voluntary personal health insurance this could also happen, of course, because in any one year even a very large contributor might receive benefits in excess of his or her contribution. But this sort of excess is in part controlled by the variation in cover which the system permits – only those who choose to pay the sort of premiums which cover, say, liver transplants, can end up subsidizing liver transplants. This means in reality that the rich subsidize the rich and the poor, whereas the poor only subsidize the poor. And of course anyone, rich or poor, can avoid the risk of subsidizing others by not taking part in the scheme (at a cost of security against ill health, of course).

The main point, however, is that under this system each individual pays insurance against the possibility of his or her own ill health according to a personal assessment of risk and value, and this includes the risk and value involved in the system itself. This makes it a system which satisfies the requirements of the freedom argument. But secondly, under the free system, there will in fact be much less chance of the poor subsidizing the rich at any point, and consequently, those who wish to protect the interests of the poor have good reason in principle to reject a compulsory socialized system and prefer that which the freedom argument has already led us to favour.

But what of the indigent, those who cannot afford health insurance? Are they simply to be ignored, as they would be under a private system? Here we need to underline the fact that the root of the problem is not lack of health insurance, but lack of money to buy it with. Nothing in this chapter rules out the desirability of supplying the destitute with money. The question is whether or not to supply them with health insurance, and the reason for not doing so is that health insurance represents a choice of values which the individual should be left free to make. In our imaginary society it may well be that there is good reason to increase the incomes of the poorest by £100 per annum. What there is not good reason to do is to assume that the most valuable way in which this increase might be spent is on health insurance, and to give it in the form of state health benefits, therefore, instead of money. It is the individual who has a right to decide, and is usually in the best position to decide, what the most valuable way to spend any extra income would be.

This system of meeting the needs of the indigent does carry with it the possibility that there would still be people who spend the extra money they receive on something other than health insurance and end up having no cover when they need it. There is no reason to think that in a free society there will be many such people, or that they will go ignored, since people are also at liberty to run charity hospitals where treatment is given without charge, as they have at most times and places. But certainly, a free society is one in which people are free to destroy themselves, and with that freedom goes responsibility too. For some reason, this is a possibility that many people are highly reluctant to permit, and they therefore continue to resist arguments which lead to the conclusion that the provision of health care is a matter that should be in the hands of the individual whose health it is (granting of course that special provision must be made for children and other vulnerable groups). Surprisingly, those who are unwilling to allow individuals freedom in matters of health will just as eagerly insist that they must have that freedom in matters of morality. And yet, as we shall see in the next chapter, the issues at stake are very similar.

6

Moral Standards and the Law

Liberal individualism of the sort we have found good reason to accept has a wide following in contemporary social philosophy, but it does not have so very long a history. In fact, it was only during the nineteenth century that it began to win widespread acceptance, and it was during that century that attention was first focused upon the issue which presents it with its greatest challenge – the relation between law and morality.

Law is an instrument of government and the state and, like many instruments of state, sooner or later it involves coercion, forcing people to do things against their will. It is one of the principal tenets of liberal philosophy that the state must respect the individual's sphere of autonomy, that part of his or her life where he or she alone has a right to decide what shall and shall not be the case. But for quite a time, philosophers have also held that morality is the sole concern of the individual whose morality it is, and from these two propositions it seems to follow immediately that the law has no business enforcing moral standards. Yet, viewed from another angle, this third proposition appears unacceptable. If we agree, as most of us will, that certain sorts of behaviour are morally repellent, it is difficult to accept that the law should stand idly by and do nothing to prevent them. And in its turn this leads to the conclusion that there must be something wrong with the liberal philosophy which suggests that it should.

This issue first surfaced in the nineteenth century, but it is still very much alive today. Those who think immoral some or all of pornographic books and films, homosexual relationships, incest, and racialist or anti-feminist rhetoric generally think that the law *ought* to take a stand and forbid them. To see whether there are convincing grounds for such a belief, and whether liberal individualism really does founder on the issue of law and morality, we need to look first at the roots and the basis of the dispute.

JOHN STUART MILL AND THE HARM CONDITION

The name most famously associated with the attempt to divorce law and morality is that of John Stuart Mill, a nineteenth-century English philosopher. Mill wrote a celebrated essay entitled 'On Liberty', in which he argued that

the sole end for which mankind are warranted, individually or collectively, in interfering with the liberty of action of any of their number, is self-protection. That the only purpose for which power can rightfully be exercised over any member of a civilized community, against his will, is to prevent harm to others. His own good, either physical or moral, is not a sufficient warrant. He cannot rightfully be compelled to do or to forbear because it will be better for him to do so, because it will make him happier, because, in the opinion of others, to do so would be wise, or even right. These are good reasons for remonstrating with him, or reasoning with him, or persuading him or entreating him, but not for compelling him. ('On Liberty', chapter 1)

Mill's view met with a good deal of criticism in its day, some of which we will examine, but over the years it has come to win widespread acceptance in the Western world. Even those who think that the law *should* forbid the production and distribution of pornographic literature, for instance, generally concede either that this is not because of its immorality so much as the fact that it causes harm, or that the fact that it causes harm is what makes it immoral. Either way, they have accepted Mill's dictum, that the only good ground for the law to intervene is the causing of harm to others, a principle sometimes known as 'the harm condition'.

It is widespread agreement on the necessity of the harm condition which explains why arguments about pornography – the portrayal of explicit or perverted sex and gratuitous violence on the television, in magazines and so on – often makes appeal to and even stimulates social research into its effects. The number of such studies conducted in Europe and North America is enormous, but I think it is true to say that not one has produced clear and indisputable evidence, or even clear but disputable evidence, of a link between the availability of pornographic 'art' and the incidence of antisocial behaviour.

This failure is only decisive, however, if first we accept Mill's principle that harm to others is the sole ground upon which the law can act against individuals. If in fact there are other perfectly good grounds upon which the law may forbid certain kinds of behaviour, the fact that the production and distribution of pornography causes no harm, if it is a fact, will be insufficient to show that the law should let it alone.

The question is, then, whether the best or only reason for making something against the law is that it causes harm to others. It is useful here to employ a distinction that philosophers make in many different contexts, the distinction between necessary and sufficient conditions. A necessary condition is something which *must* be satisfied before something else can obtain. A sufficient condition is something which, if satisfied, is *enough* for something else to hold. So for example, a functioning heart is a necessary condition for life – no one can live whose heart is not functioning – but it is not a sufficient condition, because there are other bodily malfunctions which can lead to death.

Using this terminology we see that the harm condition admits of two interpretations – that causing harm to others is a necessary condition, and that it is a sufficient condition for making something against the law. In other words, we can believe that behaviour *must* cause harm before we can properly outlaw it, and/or that if behaviour causes harm this is *enough* to justify its being against the law. The question is whether either proposition is true.

Harm as a necessary condition

The simplest way of dealing with this issue is to think of possible sorts of behaviour, to ask whether they cause harm and, if so, to ask whether they are the sorts of thing we would want to make illegal. Consider first the question 'Must something cause harm to be against the law?'. Once we think about actual causes it is obvious that the answer is 'no'. For example, it seems quite reasonable for the law to forbid the sexual molestation of very small children, and yet this may not, and quite often does not, harm them. People tend to dispute this example and assert, without reason, that sexual molestation *will* invariably cause harm, but if the sort of case we have in mind is the adult who fondles the sexual organs of six-month-old babies, this assertion is quite implausible. At any rate obviously it is *possible* that such a child is unharmed, and the point to stress is that, *whether or not* harm is caused by it, there seems good reason for the law to forbid the sexual molestation of small children. (Just what this reason is we will come back to.)

Once we get started, we can easily furnish ourselves with further examples. Take privacy. The peeping tom need do me no harm. His fault is that he invades my privacy, and privacy is something which I can reasonably call upon the law to defend. Again, there are harmless nuisances, such as loud music, which *need* do me no harm but against which I can have a legitimate complaint. Theft can be harmless – a millionaire is in effect unharmed by the theft of one of fifty-five televisions which he or she never uses and doesn't miss. Even serious crimes like rape can be harmless. No doubt most people are harmed psychologically or physically by rape, but this is not an essential feature of the crime (the victim might be raped while drugged and be unaware of it). Yet no one (I suppose) would argue that someone whose body had been used for sexual purposes without their consent, but who had not been harmed, has no cause for complaint.

The point of these examples is *not* to show that because these things may be harmless, the law should allow them. On the contrary, the argument turns on the belief that they *ought* to be against the law, but if they ought, then the causing of harm cannot be a necessary condition of making something illegal.

Harm as a sufficient condition

But neither is it a sufficient condition. It is not enough to point to something's being harmful to show that it ought to be against the law, because there are a great many activities which any society must permit which cause other people harm. Take trade, for instance. My commercial success may well be the cause of your commercial failure, and in this way I may have done you serious financial harm. But this could not carry the implication that successful trading in commercial competition should be made illegal, or life could hardly go on at all. Here again it is easy to think of a great many different examples in which harm is undoubtedly caused to others, but where there should be no question of illegality. It is not hard to imagine a scientist publishing a research paper only to have another scientist demonstrate its weaknesses and errors in public, thereby badly damaging the career prospects of the first. The first scientist is seriously harmed, but this is just not the sort of harm we want the law to forbid.

These examples illustrate that the causing of harm is not a sufficient condition for legitimately making something against the law. This might be doubted by anyone who thought that the 'harms' illustrated here – financial harm, harm to one's career – were harms in a rather special sense. Surely, it might be said, the direct causing of grievous bodily harm is always a good reason for making something illegal. But this is not so. Someone may lawfully cause another serious physical harm, even death, if the action takes place in a boxing ring. He may not do so lawfully, of course, in the street outside, for this would be assault. The salient difference, however, is not in the degree of harm caused – it seems likely that boxers cause each other more long-term harm than street muggers cause their victims – but in the fact that the boxer *consents* to the harm while the mugger's victim does not.

This last example suggests something very important, that what matters is not harm but *consent*, and earlier examples bring this out. The adult or child who is sexually molested may not be harmed, but he or she is *wronged*, because the molester *had no right* to do what he did, however harmful or harmless. Similarly, the millionaire is not harmed in any significant way, but even so the thief has done him or her a wrong, since the car belonged to the millionaire and not to the thief. From these and countless other examples it follows that I may not have certain things done to me without my consent, whether or not they cause me harm, and this as we shall see is an important conclusion for the subject of this chapter.

MORALIZING THE LAW

The argument of the preceding section demonstrated that the causing of harm is neither a necessary nor a sufficient condition for making something against the law. From this it follows that other reasons can legitimately be advanced, and this raises the possibility that an action's immorality might be one good reason for making it illegal. Why should the mere fact that an act is morally repellent not be a sufficiently good reason for making it illegal? The idea that it is is usually called 'moralizing the law'.

This question, in fact, was raised against Mill in his own day. One of his most vociferous critics was a judge called James Fitzjames Stephen (brother of Leslie Stephen, the father of Virginia Woolf), who wrote a book entitled *Liberty, Fraternity, Equality* in which he attempted to refute the claims of *On Liberty* as well as some other of Mill's writings. Stephen employed a very simple and straightforward argument which he thought Mill's liberal approach to morality would be unable to withstand. It was this.

If it is a good thing to prevent immoral behaviour and promote morally good behaviour, which by the very meaning of the terms 'moral' and 'immoral' it must be, then this is something we ought to do when we can. But such reasoning holds regardless of the nature of the means, and if the law can be used effectively to promote morality and prevent immorality, we ought to so use it.

This is an argument which, on the face of it, is hard to fault, and simple examples can be used to demonstrate its force. In the nineteenth century bear-baiting, bull-baiting, cock-fighting and dog-fighting were common pastimes from which working people derived a good deal of pleasure. Indeed the pleasure they derived, given the misery of many of their lives, probably outweighed the pain the animals suffered. But deriving pleasure from the spectacle of dumb animals forced by fear and hunger to tear each other apart was thought by many of the middle classes then, as now, to be immoral. On this ground alone they caused laws to be passed against these, and it seems right and proper that they should have. We might, of course, try to find some other ground on which to forbid blood sports (animal rights, perhaps), but even if it were clear (which it is not) that these were not themselves moral grounds, the plainest and and most simple defence of these laws seems to be that which accords with Stephen's conception of law and morality – if behaviour is immoral, as this is, and the law can stop it, as it can here, it should.

It is important to note that Stephen's argument does not imply that the law should require or forbid everything that morality requires or forbids, since it makes crucial reference to effectiveness. The law, according to Stephen, is a pretty 'rough engine', and cannot cope very well with the nice distinctions moral sensitivity often requires. Nor is it always enforceable. A law against lying might be desirable in the abstract, but it would be impracticable. Consequently there may well be many immoral actions which the law does not forbid, and should not forbid, since its doing so would have no good effect whatever.

It is easy to see how Stephen's argument would work in the pornography debate. If producing and watching films which depict defenceless animals being tortured sadistically, or young children being gang-raped, is immoral, and if the law can stop or at least reduce this sort of thing by inflicting stiff penalities on those who go in for it, then surely it should do so. What reason could there be *not* to?

Faced with this argument those who are unhappy with the idea of moralizing the law usually retreat into a sort of scepticism and deny that there is anything immoral about any of these things anyway. Or they suggest that there is no way of determining the matter. Who, they say, is to decide what is immoral? Those who watch pornographic films obviously do not share the morality of those who disapprove of them. This means that there is more than one morality in society, and even if Stephen's argument cannot be faulted as it stands, it gives us no reason to prefer one morality over another.

It is a mark of the close relation between this issue and the theoretical foundations of liberal social philosophy that in common speech those who take either of these lines – that there is no morally wrong sex or that there are different, irreconcilable but equally 'valid' moralities of sex – are generally called 'liberal'. Reflection will show, I think, that in this common speech is only partly correct. The belief that there is no place in law for moral censorship of this sort is both well founded and truly liberal, but the reasons advanced for it are not.

Moral scepticism

The two views just outlined may be called, respectively, moral scepticism and moral pluralism. Moral scepticism is a name given to the view that there is no moral right and wrong, either in some particular context such as sexual relations, or in general. People who hold this view often think that though people speak easily enough of moral right and wrong and think that they are referring to a special sort of feature that behaviour can have, they are merely expressing personal likes and dislikes, or in the strongest cases admiration and revulsion. So, for instance, a 'liberal' view of sex is often thought to be one which thinks that so-called sexual 'morality' is a hangover from the past, and that sexual orientation and behaviour are not significantly different from matters of taste. If such a view is correct, of course, there is no more reason to make homosexuality, adultery, or pornography illegal than there is to force everyone to choose the same variety of cheese.

Not everyone is as sceptical as this, and indeed most moral sceptics are sceptical only about sexual morality. Those who think that there is no moral right or wrong about extra-marital sex, incest or homosexuality are often very unlikely to take this attitude to cruelty towards children or animals, despoliation of the natural environment, war or the employment of nuclear deterrents. But in any case selective moral scepticism cannot be the answer to our difficulty. The general issue we are concerned with here is not restricted to questions about homosexuality or pornography. It concerns morality *as such*, and what the attitude of the law should be to behaviour that is immoral. Consequently, we cannot avoid the issue by being moral sceptics about just some things, such as sexual conduct, partly because the issue will continue to arise in other areas. But even more importantly, the sceptic, while disagreeing that sexual conduct is subject to moral right and wrong, is effectively conceding to those who want to moralize the law that moral views of this sort *can* in principle be legitimately enforced by law, whereas the true liberal position, for which Mill wanted to argue, is that even if homosexuality *is* truly immoral, it still ought not to be against the law. Partial moral scepticism, the so-called liberal attitude to sex, does nothing to secure this far more wide-reaching claim.

If, on the other hand, we were to embrace total moral scepticism, declaring nothing whatever to be either morally right or morally wrong, the issue would not so much be solved as disappear, but in a wholly unsatisfactory way. *No one* thinks, or has ever thought, that the law can reasonably make behaviour illegal for no reason at all, and if wholesale moral scepticism were true, this would be what the legal enforcement of morality would be. But by dissolving the dispute in this way all the moral sceptic has done is to shift the argument to another place. Those who think the law should forbid pornography and so on will now simply argue that the *scepticism* is false, and, as with partial scepticism, they will have won the basic argument that if there *were* moral rights and wrongs, these could rightly be embodied in the law.

An alternative and probably more popular view than moral scepticism is moral pluralism. This holds, not that there is no moral right or wrong, but that different people can legitimately differ about which things are morally right and which morally wrong, so that there is no one morality. Thus, some people sincerely believe that homosexuality is morally wrong, and others equally sincerely believe it is not. To ask the law to enforce morality is to ask it to decide between these two views when there is no basis for doing so. Both are moral views, held with equal sincerity by members of the same society, and must be treated equally by the law which everyone, after all, is obliged to obey.

Moral pluralism

Moral pluralism has the advantage of being in accord with recent history as it is generally perceived to have developed (though not perhaps as it actually was). When Christian morality was in the ascendant, it was widely believed that extramarital sex was immoral. Now, with the relative weakening of Christianity in the West, this belief is no longer dominant, and many people take the view that there is nothing wrong with extramarital sex on the part of couples who know and agree to what is going on. Christian morality has not disappeared, however, and what we are faced with is not one morality of sex, but two. The position is further complicated by the extensive movement of Asian and African peoples during this century. Islamic morality, with its own attitudes to sex, alcohol and so on, which at one time could be ignored by Western legal systems, is now the preferred morality of a sizeable proportion of many European populations.

But moral pluralism is, in the long run, no more relevant to the issue of this chapter than moral scepticism. Even if we agree that on some issues people do sincerely disagree about what is moral and what is immoral, and that upon these issues it is impossible to arrive at a consensus which the law might enforce, we are left with the problem of deciding what the attitude of the law should be where there is a moral consensus. Mill's argument, however unsatisfactory, aimed at the moral freedom of the individual, the freedom, it is sometimes said, to go to hell on one's own. The most important feature of Mill's 'one simple principle' is that it sets a limit to what individuals may legitimately be *compelled* to do, not what they may be advised or persuaded to do. This means that there can be good reasons, moral and non-moral, for individuals to behave in one way rather than another, but which are not the right sorts of reason to justify compelling them. Both moral scepticism and moral pluralism are in effect unable to make this distinction. They are not claiming that moral reasons are the wrong sorts of reason to base laws on, but that in certain areas, sexual conduct being the most notable, there are no such reasons.

Self-regarding and other-regarding actions

To see the force of this inability we should look at another sort of case altogether. Mill, in elaborating his principle, employs a distinction between self-regarding and other-regarding actions. He wants to distinguish between those actions which affect only the individuals who perform them and those that affect others as well. It is only other-regarding actions, he thinks, with which the law can legitimately concern itself. Individuals have a sovereign right to decide whether or not to perform those actions which affect only themselves. 'Someone's own good, whether physical or moral, is not a sufficient warrant for compulsion.'

In chapter 2 we saw good reason to attribute to individuals this fundamental right, but the limitation it generates on what we may compel other people to do is not confined to the law. Medicine and health often provide the clearest examples of the point Mill had in mind. I may be advised by my doctor to give up smoking for the sake of my health, or advised to have an operation which will prolong my life, and in making these recommendations the doctor may be telling me no more than the truth; smoking is indeed harming me, the operation really is essential. Yet the truth of neither claim is sufficient warrant for the doctor to force me to follow his recommendation. The choice is mine by right, and mine whether or not I make the right choice.

The belief that, because doctors nearly always know best which course of treatment is most advisable, it is they who should decide what treatment their patients will and will not undergo is known as medical paternalism. Paternalism of this sort is not uncommon among doctors and nurses, but in most places to act upon it would in fact be contrary to the law. A doctor who performed an operation on a patient without the patient's consent would in normal circumstances be guilty of assault, even the doctor correctly believed it to be for the patient's good. Medical paternalism is a counterpart to the political paternalism discussed in chapter 2. It finds a further parallel in moral paternalism, the idea that we can compel people to do things for their own *moral* good. It is here that we will find the real objection to moralizing the law.

MORALITY AND FREEDOM

In their different ways moral scepticism and moral pluralism argue that those who want to use the law to stop others behaving immorally are wrong to do so, not because the law cannot legitimately be used to enforce morality, but just because the behaviour in question is not actually immoral, or at least not universally agreed to be immoral. What liberal individualism needs, however, is an argument to show that, even when the behaviour in question is undoubtedly immoral, the law cannot legitimately be used to prevent it.

The parallel with medical paternalism gives us a clue as to how an argument of this sort might be constructed. Consider an act of murder. Let us agree that in all but the most exceptional circumstances murdering someone is immoral. The action has two sorts of effect. First, the victim's right to life is violated and he has sustained the greatest disbenefit of all – death. But secondly, the character of his assailant is also affected – she is now a murderer, and has, as we say, this stain on her character. Everyone will agree that there is good reason to make murder illegal, but the justification for this lies with the first rather than the second sort of effect – the point is to protect potential victims, not to protect the moral character of potential murderers. If, therefore, there are any actions whose moral importance resides *solely* in their effect upon the character of those who perform them, then, though they will still be immoral, this will not be sufficient reason to make them illegal.

Actions and intentions

Many of the actions upon which attempts to moralize the law (or prevent its being moralized) focus are arguably of this kind. Suppose we agree, for the sake of the argument, that there is indeed something immoral about watching pornographic films. It cannot straighforwardly be the watching itself which is immoral, for we can imagine committees of inquiry and boards of censors watching exactly the same films, without supposing that they are thereby engaged in immoral activity. The difference is the intention with which the action is performed. The consumer of pornographic materials aims at the expression and satifaction of evil desires, whereas the censor aims at the social control of pornographic material. The difference is an important one. Those who watch pornographic films in the interests of controlling pornography are not themselves acting immorally, whereas a government that committed murder in order to control murder would itself be acting immorally.

The point to stress is the exclusively self-regarding nature of certain sorts of behaviour. The pornographer hurts only him or herself (assuming still that pornography is immoral). I am unaffected by the fact that other people are watching porno-graphic films and am no more made immoral by them than I am made a murderer by other people murdering. Furthermore, just as the physical health of the individual in a free society is, in the last resort, a matter over which the individual is sovereign, so is his or her moral 'health'. Of course, following Mill we can agree that the morally repellent nature of certain actions is good reason to warn others against them, and for trying to persuade them not to engage in them, but it is not sufficient reason for *compelling* them to stop, by law or any other means.

Mill thought that the sole ground upon which it was permissible to make something illegal was the prevention of harm to others, and that the criminal's own good was never a sufficient reason. But *harm* to others is neither a necessary nor a sufficient reason for making something illegal. We can now see that it was only by making specific reference to harm that Mill went wrong. The important distinction is between self and others. Only the protection of others, whether from harm or something else (such as the violation of rights), can provide a good reason to make something illegal, never the protection of the individual's own good. This revised principle, I believe, captures both the spirit of Mill's *On Liberty* and a fundamental tenet of liberal individualism, but there are other problems which it encounters and which we must now look at.

Liberal morality

We have seen that liberalism makes it a fundamental principle that self-regarding actions are the business of the individual alone. One criticism that has been made of this principle suggests that it is empty, since in practice there are no such actions; every action affects somebody else. The individual who refuses to have a life-saving operation, for instance, may leave other members of the family destitute. How then can we call this action self-regarding?

To this criticism there is a reply. What matters is the intention behind the law, rather than the effect of its application. For instance, it is perfectly reasonable to force a cure upon someone who has a highly infectious disease, provided that this is done in order to protect others and not in order to cure the victim. Of course, protecting others, in this case, will involve curing him or her, but this does not alter the fact that the intention behind the action is other-regarding, and hence complies with the basic principle.

Though this reply seems reasonable enough, in fact it re-opens the door to moralizing the law, because it would appear to permit just the sort of laws that liberals, in the name of this principle, have objected to. Take homosexuality. Suppose we agree for the sake of argument that homosexuality is immoral. Consistently with the revised version of the principle we could make it illegal, not in order to improve the moral character of homosexuals, but to protect the moral well-being of others. Homosexuals, by their example, may lead others into homo-sexuality, just as those with typhoid may pass it on to others. Or to take another example, the production and free distribu-tion of pornographic magazines could be prohibited, not for the sake of those already hardened in immoral ways, but to prevent the corruption of the young; and so on.

Arguments of just this kind, in fact, were brought against liberals when they fought for religious freedom. Those who burned heretics at the stake sometimes claimed that it was not the salvation of the heretic that concerned them, but the salvation of those the heretic might mislead. If we try to oppose them by arguing that the law can only be properly used for the protection of others, we are conceding that their actions are legitimate, since their avowed intention was to protect others from the activities of the heretic.

The only other possible response seems to be sceptical, the response that there is nothing to protect others from, that there is neither salvation or damnation; and this is why liberalism has sometimes been thought the enemy of true religion. Similarly, in response to those who want to protect others from becoming homosexuals, it seems that opposition can only be based on the belief that there is nothing to protect them from, that homosexuality is not morally wrong. To avail oneself of this response, it should be obvious, is to return to the moral scepticism (at least about sexual morality) which we saw reason to reject. Perhaps, then, we should reconsider that rejection.

Morality in a free society

At an earlier stage in the argument moral scepticism was rejected on the grounds that it effectively conceded the principle that the law may legitimately be moralized. This concession is a weakness, however, only if there is some basis for thinking that the law need not and should not be moralized, and it is just such a basis that the liberal principle of protection for others is supposed to supply.

But does it? The principle tells us that the law ought to be used only to protect others. What sort of a principle is this? It could not itself be a legal one, since it is meant to determine what the law ought to be. But then it must be a moral principle of some sort, and of course this means that liberalism, far from keeping law and morality apart, is putting a moral principle at the heart of the law. Thus, under the guise of making the law neutral with respect to different moral codes, it is in fact building it around one preferred moral code. What critics of liberalism have often suspected turns out to be true – liberalism implies the rejection of many traditional moral beliefs.

There is, it seems to me, no widely agreed answer to this criticism. One possibility is to concede that, at bottom, liberal individualism is indeed a moral rather than a political doctrine, and to argue that it is morally preferable to its rivals. Such an argument would undoubtedly be based upon the fundamental importance of individual autonomy. But quite how it would go, and whether it would be successful, are difficult matters, the details of which cannot be dealt with here, though the sort of consideration that might be brought and the way it would proceed can be guessed at from the discussion of this important notion in chapter 2. What is needed to complete the topic of this chapter, however, is some indication of how, having made this concession, liberalism might still protect moral and religious freedom.

We saw that those who want to moralize the law can argue that they are acting to protect the moral well-being of others. Similarly, those who want to regulate religious belief by law could argue that they want to protect people from error. But for whom is such protection necessary? Wholehearted assent to religious doctrines can only come about by the considered, self-determined reflection of the individual. True, in a society where such reflection is uncommon, law and custom may help to make people unthinkingly accept what they have always been told, and possibly if what they have been told is true, this is better than total ignorance. But the *religious* value of such belief is questionable; unthinking acceptance of conventionally accepted doctrines does not constitute an individual's journey towards the divine.

Such, at any rate, is a familiar view of religious belief, one which makes an appearance in all the major religions. It stresses the necessity of 'inner' activity to true religion – confession, repentance, faith, hope and love – so that in an ideal world each individual would assent to (or dissent from) religious doctrines of his or her own free will and after personal thought and reflection. But it is just such a world that political liberalism aims to secure, one in which the autonomy of each individual is protected and respected fully enough to make this sort of reflection and assent (or dissent) possible. From this it follows that a liberal society is both one in which religious laws are unnecessary, and one in which true religion can flourish.

Something of the same sort is to be said about morality. If homosexuality is indeed morally wrong, then the ideal world is one in which individuals see this for themselves and act, or fail to act, not from fear of legal punishment or social censure, but from clear-headed, self-determined moral assessment. Thus, in such a world, laws regulating homosexuality would not be needed. And the same sort of argument can be applied to pornography and other actions of a generally self-regarding sort.

One obvious counter-objection to this line of thought is that people as we find them are simply not sufficiently mature for this degree of freedom, and that in the real world many will in fact be corrupted. Such a reply overlooks the earlier suggestion that it is best to think of social philosophy as the attempt to formulate the principles of as good a society as any we could aim at, rather than a set of principles for ruling an imperfect world. In other words, if in asking what the principles of a good society are we are asking what sort of society we ought, in the ideal case, to aim at, the answer is plain: one in which individuals are capable of mature and considered decisions on moral and religious matters and are not, therefore, susceptible to fads and other corrupting influences. If so, we can conclude that such a society is one in which the law would not be moralized.

It should be said, however, that there is at least one group, even in an ideal world, whose members cannot be expected to be protected from corrupting influences by their own maturity, namely children. And indeed it is to the protection of children that the enemies of pornography, promiscuity and so on often appeal. Might we not be justified in using the law to protect the moral character of individual *children*?

Since this is the second chapter to end with a question about the protection of children in a free society, it is perhaps time to tackle the issue directly.

7

Children in Society

In chapters 2 and 3 we concluded that the sort of society it would be best to have is one which gives pride of place to the rights and interests of individuals. The basis of this conclusion lay in the claims of individual autonomy, an important part of which gives each individual the sole right to decide certain matters for him or herself. Upon these matters society cannot rightfully override individual choice, and this restriction applies not just to the law, but also to the pressure of public opinion and social convention, which can often operate against the individual even more effectively and oppressively. In chapters 4, 5 and 6 we have been concerned to work out the implications of this conclusion for various aspects of social policy, to decide just what these matters are, what social structures best realize freedom of individual choice, and what steps may be needed to promote the ideal of individual freedom.

But though it is of the greatest importance to scrutinize social arrangements from the point of view of the freedom they allow mature individual citizens to direct their own lives, this is not the only point of view from which a critical examination of society is required. There are many members of society who are not mature, and are incapable of self-direction. The most obvious groups are children, the senile, the mentally handicapped and the insane. To these groups, a society which gave them the degree of freedom that is the right of the mature adult would be a disaster, one in which they would inevitably suffer or perish, and social arrangements which offered them no protection would rightly be condemned. Conversely, of course, from the fact that these members of society are not equipped for freedom it also follows that their lives may legitimately be directed by others in a way that would be quite objectionable if applied to normal adults.

A familiar way of putting this point employs the by now familiar ideas of autonomy and paternalism. Autonomy is respected in any society where individuals take responsibility for themselves and are free to make a success or a mess of their own lives. In a paternalistic society, on the other hand, the welfare of individuals is paramount, and social controls limit their freedom just as far as is necessary to protect them from themselves. Using this terminology we can say that while society should in general respect the autonomy of the individual, there are at least some groups towards which it should be paternalistic. Two sets of questions arise, therefore, in addition to any considered so far. First, what steps will the state in a good society take to protect and promote the interests of those of its members who cannot take the full range of decisions for themselves? And second, who should exercise the right to decide for them?

Children, the senile, the mentally handicapped and the insane are not the only vulnerable groups in a free society, but instead of extending the list of groups to be considered, I propose to limit the discussion of this chapter to an examination of the proper place of children. This is by far the largest of these groups, and also the most important, partly because every member of society is a child at one time or another and most will have children of their own, and partly because throughout the modern Western world a great deal of control is in fact exercised over the lives of children and minors, not just by their families, but by the state in the name of society. Moreover, there is a tendency for such control to increase as societies become ever more highly literate and technological.

For these reasons the place of children in society is of the greatest importance. I shall ask and try to answer three questions. First, when does a child become an adult, or in more legal language, what is the age of majority? Secondly, who should have control over the lives of children and take important decisions for them? Thirdly, is there good reason to compel children to go to school?

THE AGE OF MAJORITY

Most societies have had some generally agreed idea of the age at which children finally become adults and attain the right over, as well as the responsibility for, their own affairs. Few societies, however, have picked upon the same age as the age at which children become adults. Between societies and cultures there is great diversity – in Britain there is a tradition of people celebrating twenty-first birthdays as something special, while Jews of all nationalities celebrate the thirteenth birthday (for boys) as their bar mitzvah – but even within one society or culture views on this point have differed from period to period. Indeed diversity of opinion about the age of majority is even greater than has so far been suggested, because in some societies (increasingly our own) there is no one point in the life of the individual which is celebrated as *the* occasion on which he or she 'comes of age'. In these societies, maturity in different things is reached at different ages.

Where the idea of an age of majority, whether single or multiple, does operate, very often this is reflected not just in social conventions, but also in the law, which lays down an age at which it is permissible to engage in sexual intercourse, or marry, or vote, drive, leave school and so on. Here too there may be no one age of majority, but a variety of regulations permitting full participation in different activities at different ages. In Britain, for instance, children cannot leave school before sixteen, drive before seventeen (except for tractors on farms), and vote before eighteen.

These variations are of some significance, as we shall see, but there is a single idea behind all of them – that age is a measure of competence and that, in each of the examples just given, an individual is unfit to engage fully in that activity, and hence should not be allowed to, before he or she has reached a certain age. This consideration – that age brings maturity and competence with it and hence can be used to distinguish between those who are and are not rightly subjected to paternalistic control – should be distinguished from the more general idea that individuals need to have a certain degree of competence in or knowledge about sexual, political and many other activities before they can be allowed to engage fully in them. We need not dispute the latter in order to call in question the former. Indeed it is especially important that the two ideas be kept separate, since whatever the relation between 'being competent to' and 'being permitted to', it is on grounds of *age* that large numbers of people (the majority in very youthful societies) are often prevented by the state, by their parents and by social convention from doing as they, upon consideration, think best. If such widespread restriction on freedom is to be justified, we must be satisfied that the idea upon which it rests – that age is a measure of competence – is sound.

Arguments against age-limits

Some people have thought that it is not. They reason as follows. Individuals mature at different rates, and sometimes an individual will hardly mature at all in certain respects (some people remain childish to the end of their days). Conversely, some people mature long before others, and precocity of this sort is especially marked, perhaps, in matters requiring intellectual competence. But this means that you can take any age-limit you like, for any activity you like, and there will always be people *below* the age-limit who, because they have matured earlier, are *more* competent than some who are *above* it. If so, there will be things that they are forbidden to do, on the grounds of immaturity, which they are in fact more competent to do than many of the people who are already permitted to do them. What this shows is that *any* specific age-limit will include some people who are incompetent and exclude some who are competent. But since the justification for restricting individual freedom in accordance with age-limits is supposed to be that they provide a dividing line between the competent and the incompetent, this shows that they are in fact without justification.

It is not hard to illustrate the sort of thing that the critics of age-limits have in mind. In most countries thirteen- and fourteen-year-olds cannot vote or take any official part in political affairs. This exclusion from politics is usually made on the grounds that children and minors are too young to understand the complex issues involved or to feel a proper responsibility for the task. Yet we know very well that, however unsuited they may be, they cannot be any less well informed or any more irresponsible than a fair number of adult voters, and sometimes even than the occupants of public office.

Or again, consider the consumption of alcohol. Here too the assumption is that children and minors are too young to appreciate both the immediate effects and the long-term consequences of drinking. But social statistics show quite clearly that large numbers of adults are incompetent in this respect.

The examples could be multiplied. What they show, on the face of it, is that we should reject age–limits because, as a way of giving and withholding permission on the basis of competence and maturity, they are quite arbitrary. There is no age of maturity, and since the mere passage of years is no guarantee of increased competence or responsibility, we should approach the matter of competence and incompetence directly. If what matters is not that individuals have reached some age or other, but that they be mature and responsible enough to take important decisions for themselves, then we should abandon the idea of an age of majority and institute tests of competence and maturity instead.

This line of thought is a plausible one, and indeed we can strengthen its appeal, I think, by pointing out that we are already quite familiar with other sorts of competence testing. In many countries, those who want to become naturalized citizens are required to take political knowledge tests, designed to ensure that they have knowledge enough to allow them to vote intelligently, before being allowed to do so. Similarly, permission to use a gun, drive a motorcar, fly an aeroplane, or practise medicine is often controlled by competence testing. Moreover, such testing usually runs alongside an age-limit – before a certain age flying an aeroplane may be forbidden by law, but past that age it may be permissible only upon passing a flying test.

Such familiar facts make competence testing seem less of a novelty and they also serve to point up further the apparent absurdities of age-limits. Take the last example. If a man of thirty cannot pass the appropriate test, he may not fly an aeroplane; if he can, he may. This is sensible only if we assume that the test really does establish the right level of competence in flying. But if it does, then *anyone* who passes it must be competent. A lower age-limit, however, would mean that a boy of twelve, who shows himself to be no less competent by that same test, will nonetheless be forbidden to fly. This is absurd.

Should we then accept the view that age-limits are absurd and in a good society would be replaced by competence tests? There is at least one line of thought which leads us to resist this conclusion, and it is, broadly, one which asks the question 'Who is to be the tester?'.

Arguments against competence testing

No one need dispute that there are many human activities where competence really can be tested, and where competence and permissibility go hand in hand. No one should be allowed to set up as a surgeon, a taxi driver or an airline pilot without being required to show that the public is not thereby being put at unreasonable risk.

But it is very important to add that no system of testing is perfect, and that even in a system of testing competence directly we may expect some of the things that the critic objects to in the arbitrary application of age-limits – that those who are competent are excluded and those who are incompetent slip by. This means that we are not replacing one system with another of a wholly higher order, but, at best, merely a rather better one.

This is assuming that competence testing has no other problems, but in fact, though we may be clear enough about flying and driving, it is much less certain whether competence is testable over a wider range of activities, and in particular the sorts of activity that are important when we are considering the move from childhood to adulthood. Deciding whether someone can drive a car safely is quite different to deciding whether someone has the emotional maturity to raise children.

This is not to say that there is no such thing as competence or maturity in these matters. Quite the contrary. There is plainly a sense familiar to all in which, for instance, a teenage boy and girl may be judged to be incompetent parents because they lack emotional maturity. What is at issue is whether, in the absence of the broad guidelines which age-limits give us, there is any clear and indisputable test for this maturity, on the basis of which permission to marry and procreate might be given or withheld. And the obvious answer seems to be 'no'.

Someone might dispute this and maintain that just such tests are regularly in use in legal systems where the fostering and adoption of children is controlled by the state. This is a topic which we will return to in the next section, but if, for the moment, the particular example is not accepted, there are plenty more to illustrate the same point. Alcohol and other drugs can be abused. An inability not just to assess but to bear in mind the larger long-term dangers of drug taking, and a tendency to be carried away by the prospect of immediate gratification, are undoubtedly marks of adolescence. Still, some adults also behave in this way, and from this we should conclude that it is not just adolescents whose behaviour in this respect should be controlled. Consequently, there may seem good reason to abandon age-limits here in preference to competence testing.

But in what would the test consist? How do we decide who is a responsible drinker? Not just on the basis of simple drunkenness. People exhibit their immaturity in different ways, and it needs a different and higher sensitivity on the part of any 'tester' to tell emotional maturity than it does to detect sufficient skill in handling a motor car.

Part of the difficulty arises from the complexity of human action. An act of the utmost childishness on the part of one person may be nothing more than a piece of frivolity on the part of another, and yet at one level be describable in just the same terms. Most human actions, especially where they involve a high degree of thought and emotion, are of a quite different order to 'failed to look in rear mirror'. But there is a further problem too. Competence testing requires competent testers, and as the subtlety and sophistication of human behaviour increases, so does the level of subtlety and sensitivity required in those who are to assess it. The difficulty for the philosophy of society, however, arises not from doubts about whether there are such people, but whether they can be selected with sufficient ease to supply a widespread system of competence testing for all members of society over a wide range of activities.

Nor, even should such difficulties prove surmountable, would this be the end of our problems. Consider a different example. By what test is *political* competence to be established? What makes a competent voter? We know very well that people can vote ignorantly and irresponsibly (though whether they should be denied the vote on these grounds is at least debatable) but it is much less easy to say what tests would uncover this incompetence. More importantly, even if we had them, and had suitable people to apply them, to introduce a system of citizenship on merit would be to create a gross imbalance of power, because the 'testers' would now have the ability to exclude individuals from the political system, and the scope that this would leave for political malpractice hardly needs to be pointed out.

This imbalance of power, which competence testing brings into existence, is important in other contexts too, including those we have been discussing. The power of social workers, or other state employees, to decide, for instance, who may and who may not marry on grounds of competence would be a very great one, liable to both intentional and unintentional abuse, and to introduce a system of 'vetting' proposed marriages would therefore bring with it risks as well as benefits, no less than a system of vetting potential voters. What this means is that, contrary to first appearances, the abolition of age-limits and their replacement by competence testing is not a straight-forward replacement of the arbitrary with the sensible, but the replacement of one set of advantages and disadvantages with another.

This puts the dispute between the two systems on a different footing, for now any rational examination of their respective merits will be an examination of their comparative costs and benefits. Against the system of age-limits impartially applied is its arbitrariness, the fact that it will almost inevitably exclude some of the right people and include some of the wrong ones. Its advantage, however, is that it leaves no scope for prejudice or malpractice on the part of those who administer it and makes it easy for individuals to see where they stand when it comes to what they may and may not do. But it is precisely the increased chance of malpractice which counts against the system of competence testing, under which individuals are too much at the mercy of the powers that be, who, we should note, may give and withhold permission quite as arbitrarily.

The advantages of age-limits

Thus far it might be supposed that the two systems we have been considering are equally good and equally bad. But in fact further consideration will show that the system of age-limits has advantages which give it a decided edge, since it is easier to see how *its* disadvantages might be minimized.

The problem with competence testing, we have seen, is that it calls for testers of special skill and unusual impartiality. To some degree, therefore, our attitude to such a system will depend upon how optimistic and how pessimistic we are about human nature. Plato supported a hierarchical society based upon merit because he supposed that the rulers of such a system could be trained up in the right way and would not be susceptible to corruption, but most people have thought this quite absurdly optimistic, partly no doubt because the training in which Plato believed was a training in mathematics and philosophy. But in our own day, many people have a similar if somewhat more fashionable belief in the powers of social work training and counselling courses, by which the assessors of social competence may infallibly be produced. My own view is that this is no less optimistic a belief than Plato's, but for the purposes of this argument it is enough to point out that the evident defects of such a system at present cannot be remedied with ease, as all are agreed. On the other hand, the defects of the age-limit system *are* fairly easily remedied.

The problem we saw was that the rationale for an age of majority is the connection between age and competence, and this connection is rather tenuous. As a result age-limits are imperfect as a guide to maturity, and to regulate behaviour by age alone means that some of the competent will inevitably, and unjustifiably, be excluded and some of the incompetent included. This defect can be exaggerated, however. Though we may be unsure how many seventeen-year-olds could responsibly decide about voting, we have no doubt about seven-year-olds. It follows that there is indeed a very general correlation with age and maturity. Furthermore, though we may think that most seventeen-year-olds would make competent voters, we might not think them competent in other matters, to decide whether or not to be sterilized, for instance. From this it follows that the general correlation between age and competence may differ from context to context, and that flexibility in the establishment of age-limits is required. Those who believe in age-limits, however, need not be committed to the view that the age-limit must be the same for everything, and may readily admit that there needs to be considerable variation in law over the age at which individuals become responsible for different aspects of their own affairs (a variation which is to be found in most legal systems, in fact).

If we combine these considerations, we can see very readily that though the arbitrariness of age-limits cannot be altogether avoided, it can be minimized by a flexible approach to them. More importantly, the attempt to minimize it is a more hopeful one than the corresponding necessity to supply competent competence testers.

Just where the age-limit for any particular activity should be drawn is not a matter philosophical argument can settle, but one which needs to be considered in the light of the conditions obtaining at different times and places. What the argument of this section has shown is that those who favour age-limits as a way of defining who is and who is not a child can successfully defend their belief (and with it the practice of most societies) against the initially plausible arguments of the critic, provided they acknowledge the need for a wide range of different age-limits, and with it, I think, an acceptance that in many places at the present time age-limits are quite improperly drawn.

PARENTS OR GUARDIANS?

Whatever reasons might be brought against the straightforward application of age-limits, there cannot be any serious doubt that there *is* such a thing as a child and that children, as a class, are in need of both supervision and protection. No young child is capable of promoting, or even of comprehending, the full range of his or her interests. Matters which will affect their lives in the most important ways have to be decided *for* them. This raises a question about who should do the deciding.

In fact, the question is one of great importance, because, though in almost all societies the presumption is that it is natural parents who should have charge of and act for the child, experience confirms that some parents look after their children's interests much better than others, and some non-parents better than parents would. Neglect and abuse of children by their natural parents is, unfortunately, a not uncommon occurrence. What this shows is that parenting is something which can be done more and less well and the mere fact that someone is a natural parent is no guarantee of good parenting. What reason is there, then, to accept the common presumption? One way of approaching this question is to look at the alternatives.

Once more it is in Plato that we find the earliest exponent of radical ideas. In his ideal Republic, children were to be taken from their mothers at birth and brought up in common. Thereby, instead of being restricted to the sort of upbringing that their parents were willing and able to give them, they could be provided with the education and training best suited to their needs and natures. The desirability, and plausibility, of the scheme depended, of course, upon Plato's general conception of goodness, knowledge and social order and not much of this is likely to be found persuasive today. But the idea of taking children away from their natural parents has continued to find favour among social visionaries up to the present day. How far it has been actually been applied by anyone, and with what effect, is a strictly empirical matter, not one that philosophy can pontificate about, but what we are concerned with here is not the effects of social experimentation so much as the moral acceptability or otherwise of the *idea* of socially appointed guardians for children and minors.

Before considering the matter directly, however, we should note that many such schemes have been advocated not so much with the interests of children in mind as with the benefit to society. In the next section some of these arguments will be examined when we look at reasons for compulsory schooling, but in this section the question at issue is whether children should be entrusted to socially appointed guardians rather than natural parents *for their own sake*, whatever the benefits to society.

There is reason to think that they should only if there is reason to think that, overall, such guardians would be better custodians of the child's interests than natural parents would be. Plato had reason to think this because he thought he knew just what such guardians needed to know for the successful raising of children, and just how this knowledge was to be imparted to them. His theory of 'the Good', however, upon which this belief depended for its cogency, is riddled with confusion and difficulty, so that there is no reason to accept any of the implied recommendations he may have drawn from it. More recent thinkers, of course, have called upon psychology (and sometimes sociology) as a better and more scientific basis for parent training, but there really is no reason to think that their theories are any more certain or their recommendations any better grounded than Plato's.

One difficulty with *any* view of this sort is that parenting is not simply a matter of education and training. Emotions enter into good parenting in crucial ways. Love is important in successful parenting and one cannot be *trained* to love one's charges. So too are pride, anxiety and so on, and none of these are to be instilled in a training course.

In fact, these commonsense observations give a clue to the reason for a presumption in favour of natural parenting – parents are more likely to love, be proud of, worry about their own children than they are about other people's, and the presence of these emotions makes for better parenting. *This* is why natural parents are likely to be better custodians of the interests and welfare of their own children than any state appointed guardians, however well trained, could reasonably be expected to be.

This is only a likelihood, however, and it remains the case that not all parents love or cherish their children. Moreover, the privacy of the family home means that where parents are bad, children are likely to suffer worse than they would in a state- or charity-run children's home. Both contentions are amply supported by almost daily evidence on the television and in the newspapers of any modern industrial society, and may also be confirmed by the records of societies past. We cannot, therefore, assume that society has no role in the guardianship of children, and if, as a general rule, children ought to be left to be brought up by their natural parents, we must also decide how, when the occasion arises, they are to be protected *from* their parents.

Licensing parents

An American philosopher, Hugh LaFollette, has recently made the interesting suggestion that we should require parents to have licences. A licence is in fact a very useful social instrument, because it allows for something in between permission and prohibition. It neither says 'You may' nor 'You may not', but rather 'You may, provided you . . .', and this middle way between outright permission and outright prohibition would appear to be just what we need. If it is a mistake to forbid natural parents as such to bring up their children, on the grounds that they should be handed over to trained guardians who will be guaranteed to look after their interests, it is also a mistake to suppose that all parents everywhere must be permitted to bring up their own children, exactly because natural parenting may put the interest of some children at risk. Licences could be used to regulate parenting in precisely the way required. Moreover, since the conditions which attach to a licence may range from the very simple to the very stringent, the system promises great flexibility in dealing with the widely different circumstances that will undoubtedly arise in a society of any complexity.

The idea of licensing parents is (in my experience) generally regarded as an unacceptable intrusion by the state into family life, something which any society should hold sacrosanct. But is this objection anything more than a prejudice against the unfamiliar, dressed up in high-sounding language? To put the matter bluntly, we accept quite happily the necessity of licences to drive, on the grounds (though not these alone perhaps) that drivers put others at risk. And we accept equally happily that *everyone* who wishes to drive must have a licence, even though we know that it is only a small minority who are likely to be a danger to others. Should we not, in consistency, also accept the necessity of licensing parents, on the grounds that children may be badly harmed by their parents, even though we acknowledge that this will happen only in a minority of cases?

We can make the idea more acceptable, perhaps, by demonstrating that it is not as novel as it at first appears. One striking difference between driving licences and parenting licences, we might think, is that the latter, unlike the former, are concerned with a highly personal part of the individual's life. But we could persist in stressing this difference only if it were not already the case in many societies that couples require a licence to marry. And it seems a small step from marrying to parenting. In fact the two are connected: in times past, before effective methods of birth control, it was virtually impossible to permit marriage and not at the same time permit procreation, and for this reason the question of procreation was often present in the minds of those who thought about the requirements of marriage. At least part of the point of the Christian table of proscribed relations (according to which a man may not marry his mother, etc.) was to ensure satisfactory procreation of children.

If this is right, there seems nothing very dramatic in the suggestion that the conditions under which people are granted marriage licences should take account both of the widespread use of effective birth control and of the increasing numbers of non-marital relationships, and that licences for parenting as well as marrying might be a sensible innovation.

Nor is the idea of vetting possible parents wholly unfamiliar. It happens all the time in the case of adoptive and foster parents. Indeed it is one of the oddities of modern society that, while no conditions are laid down in advance for natural parents, those who wish to adopt must pass the most rigorous scrutiny, usually by state-run agencies.

But the suggestion that natural parents too should require licences is even less innovatory than all that has been said so far might imply. Whilst it is true that nowhere (to my knowledge) are conditions laid down in advance for natural parents, almost every industrialized country has legal procedures by which children may be *removed* from the care of their natural parents, usually upon grounds of cruelty, abuse or neglect. In effect, this means that we already *have* the elements of licensing. There is still an important difference, however. At present the presumption is that everyone will be allowed to take charge of their children, unless they show themselves unfit to do so. Under a licensing system the presumption would be that no one will be allowed to be a parent unless they have shown themselves fit to be so.

Objections to licensing parents

We have seen reason to think that the idea of licensing parents is not such a startling novelty as we might have thought. Nevertheless, there remains the question as to which presumption is better, and how to square society's treatment of natural parents with its treatment of adoptive and foster parents. There are both practical difficulties, and difficulties of a sort already discussed in the last section, with the suggestion that the sort of scrutiny which adoptive parents commonly undergo could be extended to *all* parents.

Consider first the practical difficulties. The scrutiny of potential adoptive parents is pretty exhaustive, perhaps more so than is necessary, but it is evident that to extend it to all parents would require the creation of a bureaucracy which most societies would be unable and probably unwise to support. On top of this, there is always, as in any testing and licensing system, the certainty of mistakes. This means that we would not necessarily end up with a system under which children were better protected. But it also means that, in addition, we would run the risk of depriving innocent people of one of their greatest opportunities – having and raising their own children. Nor is this risk insignificant. Children *are* sometimes wrongly taken away from their natural parents by social workers and others in authority, and this is a source of great unhappiness and hardship.

But there are greater dangers too. Control of who may and who may not have children is a power open to abuse, and it is not difficult to see that it could most easily be abused on racial, religious or political grounds. Moreover, the number of societies in which racial and religious tensions exist suggests that the risk of these dangers being realized is considerable.

These are, of course, surmises of an empirical kind. My guess is that licensing parents is a power that we could well do without, and that even if the system functioned as well as could be expected the benefits would be marginal, but the question is one which we cannot settle without some detailed empirical investigation into particular societies. As far as social philosophy is concerned our conclusion must be that control of parenting by licence is in principle an acceptable enough system, with the elements of which we are already familiar, and the objections to which are likely to be prudential.

Summary

So far in this chapter we have considered the idea of an age of majority and its application in regulating the freedom of the individual in society. I have argued that, despite their agreed arbitrariness, there is good reason to employ age-limits as a simple way of ensuring that individuals exercise only those rights they are capable of exercising and that the introduction of direct competence testing would in most contexts be fraught with danger and difficulty. This is not to deny, however, that there is a place for tests of competence in deciding who should be permitted to do what. The argument in the first section concerned the ability of children to decide for themselves what is in their own best interests, a right which a free society will give to everyone, and concluded that age is sufficiently closely related to maturity to make the employment of age-limits defensible, and, further, that the relative ease with which these limits can be applied impartially makes them preferable to direct tests of competence.

The idea of making an individual's freedom from paternalistic control dependent upon his or her ability to past certain tests is one which individualists will always treat with the greatest circumspection, even though in some contexts – dealing with the mentally ill and mentally handicapped, for instance – something of this sort cannot be avoided. The same arguments for caution do not apply, or at least not so straightforwardly, when we consider the behaviour of individuals as it affects the freedom and welfare of others. No one who doubts the desirability of a test to decide whether or not I should in my own interests be allowed to drink, need question the desirability of a test, in other people's interest, to decide whether or not I should be allowed to perform surgery.

Tests of this sort are common, and commonly accepted as part of the proper regulation of social interaction. What the argument of this section has shown is that there is no reason *in principle* to object to the introduction of such tests for parents, and issuing permission to have children only to those who can pass them. Licensing parents would still be a far cry from removing children altogether and placing them under the guardianship of the state's appointee, a procedure which sounds to most people unacceptably tyrannical.

Yet, surprisingly, perhaps, this is to an extent just what most modern societies do, for they require parents to give over charge of their children to state appointed custodians for the larger part of most days, throughout the greater part of the year. I mean, of course, by sending them to school. It is to the defensibility of compulsory schooling that we now turn.

COMPULSORY SCHOOLING

A good society, we have seen, is one in which individuals are as far as possible given freedom and responsibility for their own affairs. In a good society, therefore, one would expect relatively few restrictions on what individuals may and may not do with their time. This test of the good society applies chiefly to its treatment of its mature adult members, and in this chapter we are concerned with other social groups, principally children and minors, to which this test does not apply so readily. Still, it is a striking fact that in almost all modern industrial societies it is as children we are most subject to social restrictions, and that the development from child to adult brings with it an enormous increase in freedom. This is primarily because we are no longer compelled to spend most of our time at school.

Compulsory schooling is such a familiar part of social life that the scale of the compulsion rarely strikes us, and the fact that it applies to children makes us less concerned about its justification. Between the ages of, roughly, five and fifteen (these vary from country to country, of course) children are obliged by law to spend most of their lives at school, whether they want to or not. Usually, the state's compulsion does not bear directly upon younger children. It is their parents who are obliged to send them to school and they would probably do so voluntarily anyway (though of course there is still the question why parents should be compelled to do so). Consequently 'Why must I go to school?' is usually given serious consideration only when it is raised by older children whose parents sympathize in part with their point of view, and since such pupils are close to leaving anyway, the question is usually shelved. Yet we have only to imagine other possibilities to see that, even in the case of younger children, compulsory attendance at some one institution day in day out for ten years (holidays apart) is something which most people would object to. No one would contemplate making daily church attendance compulsory even for small children, or compelling them to visit the supermarket every weekday, or the sports stadium or the swimming pool. What then is so special about school?

Answers to this question are of two sorts, and they reflect the fundamental division between individualism and communitarianism discussed in the first two chapters. Individualist defences of schooling concentrate on the potential benefits to the child. Communitarian defences draw our attention to the benefits for society at large. Let us consider each of these in turn.

Individualist defences of compulsory schooling

It is a commonplace that education is valuable. Without education, an individual will be seriously handicapped as an adult. A child who grows up uneducated will be deprived of a very wide range of benefits and opportunities, and this will seriously impoverish his or her adult life. More importantly from an individualist point of view, perhaps, a lack of education impairs autonomy; it is said to make us less able to decide for ourselves what career to pursue, whom to marry, whether to have children, and so on. But children, especially perhaps teenage children, are unlikely to appreciate this. They have neither the experience nor the maturity to resist more immediate pleasures and left to their own devices would probably play away the day. It is only as adults, and then too late, that they will realize what they have missed.

It is not difficult to see how this argument is intended to justify compulsory schooling. When, contrary to their wishes, society compels children to go to school, this is not an infringement of individual liberty because it is not overriding the will of an autonomous individual, but, odd though it may sound, actually enforcing it. Resistance to schooling, if there is any, comes from the child; the desire for it, it may be assumed, comes from the adult that the child will grow up to be. Thus in a sense compulsory schooling is self-imposed, and consequently it is not really a restriction on the freedom of the individual at all.

This argument has a certain appealing ingenuity, but it rests upon several important mistakes, not least its supposition that most adults are glad of the schooling they were forced to have as children. But chief amongst its errors is a mistaken assumption (one that nearly everyone makes in discussion of this issue), that education and schooling are one and the same. This is plainly false. The single most important thing that we learn is the language we speak, and yet this learning takes place before ever we get to school. Furthermore, such extra-school education continues throughout our lives as children (and beyond). By and large we learn a much larger range of useful skills and gather a great deal more usable information *outside* school than we do in it – how to buy and sell, ride a bicycle, whistle, play cards, look after animals, operate television and video, and many, many more. Every one of these is a skill we are likely to value in later life, and though we rarely need to be forced to learn these things, we might agree, as adults, that we would be glad to have been compelled to learn them if we did.

But our agreement that *education* is sufficiently valuable to warrant the compulsory education of children still leaves us without a justification of compulsory *schooling*, precisely because this great battery of education can and does take place out of school. A revised form of the individualist argument might accept that it is a mistake to identify all education with schooling, but suggest that formal schooling *is* needed for education in certain skills, and that furthermore these skills are essential to any adult in the modern world.

What could these special skills be? The obvious candidates are literacy and numeracy, the ability to read, write and deal with numbers, and certainly these are skills without which life in most modern societies is very difficult. If these are the essential benefits of schooling, however, we should not be too easily persuaded by the revised form of the argument, first of all because it is not only in schools that these things are or can be taught, and secondly because far more than literacy and numeracy is taught in most schools and pupils are required to attend long after these basic skills have been mastered. Even if we ignore the first of these points (on the grounds that in practice most children will only learn to read and write at school), and accept the claim that literacy and numeracy are essential skills for any adult in the modern world, the best we could conclude is that there is justification for a far shorter period of schooling than that which children are commonly compelled to undergo.

This limited conclusion is strengthened when we consider what it is that children do learn at school. Where the emphasis is put upon academic subjects, it is almost always impossible to argue that the curriculum, however good in itself, is fitting the pupil for life. At the very least, we can say that there are many pupils who will be better fitted for life by classes in car mechanics than by classes in trigonometry or ancient history. Can anyone seriously argue that in general individuals of thirteen and fourteen years of age should be compelled to take these esoteric subjects because they will themselves value them in the future?

Those who are not opposed to compulsory education often suppose that this point can be answered by admitting the need for greater flexibility within the curriculum and in particular the introduction of more 'relevant' subjects. But the argument that society is justified in compelling children to go to school because of what they learn there has no plausibility for *any* set of subjects beyond the most basic. Computer studies is not a more valuable subject than history to those who will have no use for computers in later life, and a knowledge of neither is essential to successful living in the modern world.

Indeed it would be very odd if any but the most basic school subjects were to prove essential in any deep or important sense, because the vast majority of mankind, hitherto and till very recently, have managed to live satisfactory lives without any schooling at all. This is not to deny that their lives might have been improved by schooling (though crucially the truth of this depends upon the sort of schooling they might have had), but only to deny that the benefits of schooling are of the right kind to justify widespread compulsion. No doubt there are many things besides schooling that we would be better off for having done, but which nevertheless we could not rightly be forced to do.

We have been asking why individual members of modern society should be compelled to go to school for so much of their early lives. The answer that it is for their own good, we have seen, is inadequate, partly because, even if education is so valuable that we can compel children to have it, this same valuation does not carry over to *schooling*. But any similar claim made directly about schooling seems very implausible when we consider first how much is learnt elsewhere, and secondly how little of what is learnt in school is likely to be essential for a satisfactory adult life. Nor is this something which might be remedied by a better curriculum. The only set of subjects that are both likely to be of vital importance to anyone and can best be acquired at school, namely basic literacy and numeracy, would justify nothing like the amount of schooling required by most societies. From these considerations it follows that individualist defences of compulsory schooling are unsuccessful. It remains to be seen whether community rather than individual centred justifications can do any better.

Communitarian arguments in favour of compulsory schooling

Sometimes people have argued that the real justification for compulsory schooling is not to be found in the needs of the individual, but in the needs of society. Societies are better off if their populations are well educated, or so it is said, and certainly it appears that a high level of literacy is characteristic of wealthy nations and a low level characteristic of poor ones. The trouble, especially in poor societies, is that conditions make it economically advantageous *in the short term* for people to put their children to work as young as possible. Consequently the much greater long-term economic advantages of education are never realized. So, the communitarian argues, if we want a prosperous society, which we all *do* want, we will want a well-educated public, and to achieve this we will have to compel people to send their children to school. To the liberal objection that individual parents and children cannot rightly be sacrificed for the sake of society as a whole, the communitarian replies that those who are compelled in this way will reap greater relative benefits, since the enhanced prosperity of their society will be worth more to those who would not otherwise have been educated than it will to others who would have been.

This line of thinking, in fact, informs a very great deal of modern social policy. People, and politicians especially, have a strong tendency to think of education in terms of society's needs – 'Germany needs more doctors' – 'Britain's need for engineers will have grown by the end of the decade' – and of educational systems as producers of industrial and commercial personnel – 'The United States is producing too many lawyers', 'There are not enough scientists coming out of the schools' – but as it stands, no argument of this sort even begins to supply a plausible basis upon which compulsory schooling could be justified. In the first place it does not seem to be true that compulsory schooling is a necessary condition of economic and political success. All the great empires of the past arose from societies in which compulsory schooling was unknown, in which schooling was almost unknown, indeed. Of course, education was not lacking in those societies, but the same point as was made against the individualist is effective here too – education is not to be identified with schooling.

Even if, following the lines of the previous argument, we agree that there are indeed basic skills which for all practical purposes must be learnt in school, and which the individual may be compelled to acquire for the sake of the social benefits this will bring, there must, as before, be serious doubt whether this could justify the compulsion to study the whole modern school curriculum. To argue otherwise, in fact, is to tread very dangerous ground. If we are justified in forcing people to acquire more than the most basic and easily acquired skills, which could not require ten years of constant schooling, we are justified in compulsion long past that point and in forcing them into higher education and further training. The claim that society needs doctors and engineers will more readily justify compelling adults to take higher education courses in the professions 'society' needs, rather than leaving them to take courses of their own choosing, than it will justify compelling children to go to primary school, where neither medicine nor engineering is taught.

In short, the belief that we are justified in compelling individuals to take educational courses because of the needs of society is likely to carry us far past the provision of schools for children, and on to wholesale central directives designed to produce the ideal workforce. As we shall see in chapter 8, there are further difficulties here about how 'society's needs' are to be determined, and by whom, but here I think enough has been said to show that communitarian attempts to justify compulsory schooling are not any more successful than their individualist counterparts.

The claim that compulsory schooling is without justification, a conclusion this section might seem to support, is striking to the point of eccentricity, so sharply does it conflict with common belief and practice. In point of fact, however, this very clear conclusion does not follow from the arguments we have been considering, which show rather that compulsory schooling on the scale with which most modern industrialized societies are familiar is in all probability unjustified. In any case, it would be absurd to suggest that schooling should be made entirely voluntary, because so fundamentally is it built into the structure of every modern society that the consequences of such a policy could be dire, both at a social and an individual level. What is not so absurd is the suggestion that the the content and length of compulsory schooling warrants close critical scrutiny, and that the possibilities and value of other sorts of education can be and usually are too easily overlooked.

8

Engineering the Good Society

We have now reached the end of this introduction to the principles of social philosophy and to their implications for some of the main areas of social policy. The general conclusion has been that a good society is in a deep sense *for* the people who live in it, and that the principles on which it is organized will protect their freedom as autonomous, self-motivated and self-directing individuals, valued as ends in themselves. This is what 'individualism' is to be taken to mean, and it carries the implication that programmes and policies which aim at social justice and social equality must ultimately be justified by the contribution they make to individual freedom. This individualist requirement also applies to the ways in which society provides for the health of its citizens, for the expression of their moral and religious concerns, and the ways in which it seeks to protect its children.

In chapter 2 we found reason to regard individualism so conceived as an emergent ideal. What this means is that our conception of society is a conception of the sort of society we should hope to have. Any conception of the good society, therefore, must be fashioned around an idea of the best possible sort of human life, and not around human lives as they ordinarily have gone. Such an approach, however, raises afresh a doubt about the realism and practicality of social philosophy, raises, in fact, the very doubt the discussion of Marx and Machiavelli was intended to dispel. Can such a high-flown and idealistic conception of society be of any practical interest? Or is it not, as Marx and Machiavelli thought, idle Utopian dreaming?

In this final chapter we need to examine these doubts once more, not now in the form that particular writers have raised them, but in a rather more general way. In doing so, we will be considering another set of problems with which social philosophy is concerned – the nature of our knowledge and understanding of societies, in short the nature of social science. Three questions are specially important here. First, how can we tell just how far short of the ideal any existing society falls? Secondly, can we use our understanding to engineer a better one? And thirdly, if social engineering is impossible, what, if anything, can social philosophy teach us?

SOCIAL SCIENCE

To act upon any conception of the good society we must first of all know the place from which we start. There is no need to alter a social system which is already as good as it can be. But how do we know how good it is? Here it is natural to look to the social sciences; just as doctors begin any course of treatment with an examination of the patient's condition based upon and informed by the language and understanding of medical science, so the social sciences might be thought to be the source of our knowledge and understanding of the existing structure and functioning of society.

But philosophers and others (including some social scientists) have often been beset by doubts at this point, and wondered whether there really is anything that can properly be called 'social science'. Of course, we must be careful how we understand this doubt. No denies that there are subjects *called* social sciences, such as economics and sociology, which form an established part of the curriculum in schools and universities across the world. What is in doubt is whether, individually or collectively, these provide us with the means of describing and explaining the behaviour of societies in anything like the same way as that in which medical science helps us to understand the human body, or astronomy helps us to understand the behaviour of stars and galaxies.

Arguments against social 'science'

To appreciate these doubts better, we need to look a little more closely at the idea of a science. The word 'science' comes from the Latin word meaning 'knowledge', and until the early part of the last century, by 'science' people generally meant nothing more than knowledge and its systematic organization. But as spectacular advances were made in physics, chemistry and biology, till they reached a degree of sophistication and explanatory power undreamt of 300 years before, the word increasingly came to be identified with the natural sciences. The result is that, while the eighteenth century would not have thought it odd to call law or theology a 'science', today a contrast is usually drawn between 'the sciences' on the one hand and 'the arts' on the other.

What is the distinguishing feature of science according to this modern classification? A number of proposals have been made. Some people have thought of science as 'objective' inquiry, and meant by this one in which questions can be settled irrespective of the values of those who investigate them, an inquiry which concerns itself with publicly ascertainable 'fact' rather than the vagaries of personal 'opinion'. Others have thought that science in the modern sense is to be characterized as the study of deterministic physical systems, systems in which causal laws operate, and regulate the things we want to study and explain. Still others have suggested that what marks science off from other sorts of study is its ability to formulate theories that hold universally, and which can be used to make accurate predictions.

There have been other suggestions too, but these three are sufficient to show how doubts about the possibility of *social* science arise. It seems pretty clear to a good many people, including a number of social scientists, that for an inquiry to be objective it must be value free, that is, something about which questions of good and bad, right and wrong, do not arise. Such objectivity, they think, is possible in the natural sciences where the subject matter to be studied – facts about the observable, physical world – is itself value free. But no study of society can achieve a similar freedom. Social 'facts' are always conceived in language that has values implicit in it. Even the specialist terms that social scientists employ – 'economic stagnation', 'social deviance' – imply value judgements; a stagnant economy is a bad one, social deviance is a rejection of society's norms. It follows, if we characterize 'science' as value free, that there can be no social science.

The same conclusion, it has been argued, follows from the second characterization of science. The behaviour of societies is made up, at least in part, of the actions of individual human beings. Human beings are not simply physical systems. They have free will, and unlike the behaviour of atoms, cells or stars, their conduct is the outcome of thought, deliberation and choice, not merely causal laws. It is not, therefore, susceptible to the same sort of analysis and explanation as the purely physical, and in consequence, though there can be social *study*, there cannot be social *science*.

Finally, the third conception of science easily generates the same conclusion. Philosophers have focused upon the theoretical and predictive character of the natural sciences. Sometimes, again appealing to free will, they have argued that human behaviour and hence the behaviour of societies cannot be predicted, but sometimes they have pointed (perhaps more tellingly) to the impressive explanatory theories that are found in all the physical sciences, and to the striking absence of anything remotely similar in the social 'sciences'. On this view, science, unlike history, say, is theoretical, and it simply is a fact about social 'science' that it has generated no theories.

The force of the arguments

Is there any force in these arguments? The first seems to make an invalid inference. Suppose, for the moment, that science is an objective, value-free inquiry, and that social science could not be value free. The inference that it cannot therefore be objective requires an additional premise: that natural science is objective *because* it is value-free. But why should values not be investigated objectively? There seems no reason in principle against it. In fact it is easy to think of lots of familiar examples of objective investigation into good and bad, right and wrong, which confirm this – good and bad methods of treating cancer, keeping wine or growing roses can be investigated, for instance, in a perfectly objective fashion. So why not other values like good and bad ways to organize society?

But even if this necessary premise were not missing, the argument as it stands misrepresents both natural science and social inquiry. On the one hand, the study of physics, chemistry or biology is *not* value free. It requires us to prefer truth to falsehood, and to examine the value of different methods of inquiry from the point of view of producing genuine knowledge. On the other hand, social study frequently requires investigation into straightforward matters of fact, where values are not in question. Social scientists might need to know whether average incomes have been rising or falling over a given period, without asking whether this is a good or a bad thing.

It seems clear, then, that the first argument gives us no good reason to doubt the very possibility of social science. What of the second argument, that societies are not deterministic systems in the way that material bodies are and cannot therefore be studied scientifically? The fault here is that there is too much generalization. Those who speak happily of 'the natural sciences' are often quite unaware of the great variety of subjects covered by this description, and hence of the important differences between, for instance, biology and physics. Biology makes extensive use of the idea of 'function' in its explanations, which physics does not, and physical theories admit of mathematical formulation in a way that biology hardly ever does. In view of these differences, it seems possible and likely that the social sciences might be more like some natural sciences than others. If we add that there is variety within social sciences too – economics uses mathematics in a way that sociology does not – there seems even less plausibility in the sweeping generalization that 'the social sciences' could not be like 'the natural sciences'. Any such contrast is plausible only so long as we are thinking of physics and anthropology, much less plausible if we are thinking of biology and sociology.

The third argument is, in my view, the most substantial of the three. It rests upon a striking difference in the *state* of natural science and social study. Whereas physics, chemistry, astronomy, zoology and the like have impressive bodies of widely accepted theories, which are used to explain many natural phenomena successfully, the social 'sciences' are almost totally lacking in substantial theories, and those that there are, are widely contested. Engels once suggested that Marx had done for the study of society what Darwin had done for the study of the animal world, but one hundred years later it is plain that the achievements of the two are not comparable at all, and this is evidenced by the fact that the status of Darwin's theory of evolution in modern biology is quite different to the status of Marx's theory in social science. Nearly all contemporary sociologists agree on the importance of Marx's theory, but they do not actually use and build upon it in the way that modern biologists use and build upon Darwin.

It is important to be clear about this difference and its significance. The claim we are considering is that real science is characterized by its ability to produce precisely formulated, wide ranging explanatory theories and that, as a matter of fact, the study of economy and society has produced no such theories. In taking this view, however, we need not be too troubled about labels. Call them social sciences if you will; this title cannot obscure the fact that there just is no counterpart in the study of societies that might serve politicians and social planners in the way that natural science serves doctors and engineers. There is nothing in any branch of the social sciences at all comparable to Einstein's theory of relativity.

The absence of theory in the social sciences

The power of this argument lies in its assertion of incontestable fact. This fact – that there are no successful theories in social science – can be explained in different ways. Sometimes it has been suggested that it results from nothing more than the comparative immaturity of the social sciences. While natural science has been developing since the days of the ancient Greeks, social science is barely 250 years old. But this explanation is not very convincing, to my mind. Those same 250 years have been long enough for the major development of most other sciences, and it is precisely over that same period that some – genetics, for instance – have both been born and developed to spectacular heights.

Relative youth, then, is too superficial an explanation. An alternative idea is that the absence of theory is no accident and arises from the nature of social study itself. There is indeed some basis for this suggestion. Theorizing in physics and chemistry very often takes the form of tested universalization. For example, Boyle's law, which describes the behaviour of gases, though it is a law about physical reality, can be stated in an abstract and wholly universal form, namely $PV = RT$ (the pressure and volume of a gas, multiplied together, will equal its temperature, multiplied by a constant for each different gas). This form allows the law to be tested by experimentation with different gases, and to be rejected or amended in accordance with the results, as indeed Boyle's Law was by Van der Waals' experiments (to read $(P-\frac{a}{V^2})\ (V+b) = RT$). Both Universalization and testing are possible because gases share essential common properties, so that it does not matter which samples of gas Boyle and Van der Waals used, or where or when their experiments too place. For scientific puposes, all gases are alike.

But arguably social phenomena are not like this, partly because the history of each society is unique, and partly because social investigation can itself influence and change social behaviour. Consider, for instance, an attempt, such as has not infrequently been made, to formulate a theory of revolutions – a theory that is to say, which will explain why revolutions take place when and where they do. Here, there may be some generalizations which, as a matter of fact, hold good for a number of revolutions, but this falls far short of universality. The English, French, American, Russian and Iranian revolutions were all revolutions against crowned heads of state, but the circumstances of each and the conceptions of the revolutionaries were so very different that that is probably the only common feature they have. Moreover, those who engaged in the Russian revolution were familiar with the French revolution and understood their own revolution in historical relation to it, and it is partly this understanding that determined their conduct. This means that some of the differences between the two are to be explained by the fact that one took place before the other, whereas the behaviour of a gas under experiment could never be affected by the fact that similar experiments had taken place before.

Philosophers have argued much further on these matters, claiming for instance that the crucial difference between social study and natural science is that the former is concerned with intentional behaviour, the latter not. I could, for instance, set myself intentionally to refute a theory of economic behaviour simply by behaving differently, but a gas cannot intend to refute Boyle's Law by altering *its* behaviour. Other philosophers have doubted if this difference is indeed crucial, but whether it is or not, there is general agreement that we do not have, and have no immediate prospect of having, social scientific theories with anything like the precision, scope or power of those which typify modern natural science. Even in the more theoretical social sciences – economics for instance – where the existence of sophisticated mathematical models might be thought to provide a counter-example – the possibility of theory has been gained at the expense of a retreat into the ideal worlds of the rational economic human being, perfect competition and so on. Whatever the interest and value of these models (and it is very considerable), they cannot be understood to be empirically testable theories of the workings of real economies.

The nature of science and social science is a large and important topic in modern philosophy, and we have only touched upon some of the main themes here. But we have seen enough to know that there are good and bad reasons for thinking that social *science* is not a promising prospect. If so, this unquestionably presents an important problem for social philosophy, but not perhaps quite the problem that it at first appears.

We began by asking how we could ascertain the truth about the social reality from which any attempt to build a good society might begin, and found reason to doubt the possibility of a social science that would supply us with the requisite knowledge. But in fact what we have discovered is a limitation upon the *theoretical* advances that social inquiry could make (or at least is likely to make), and though this is important, as we shall see in the next section, there is still room for valuable, objective social investigation. The fact that there is little or no scope for universally applicable theories does not prevent the study of societies from providing the means of determining the truth about existing societies. Though we may have reason to doubt the possibility of a General Theory of Employment,

Interest and Money (the title of John Maynard Keynes's most famous book), this does not carry the implication that we can never discover whether unemployment is rising or falling. Similarly, though general theories of criminal behaviour may be so limited in their application to particular times and places that there is little reason to call them theories at all, this does not mean that piecemeal explanation of the rise or fall in crime here or there cannot have interest and value.

Nor should this non-theoretical social science be looked down upon. To establish clearly and straightforwardly the truth about any society or economy is in fact a complex business that may require a high level of intellectual sophistication. For instance, much information about contemporary society relies upon sampling and the gathering of statistics. But sampling and the interpretation of statistics is a difficult and highly complex affair, which requires, amongst other things, grasp of computational techniques no less intricate that those which natural science employs. To suppose otherwise is to confuse the non-theoretical with the simple, and this is a profound mistake.

But for all this, the non-theoretical character of social science is a problem for social philosophy because it raises a doubt about the possibility of social engineering. If the best we can know is the state society is currently in, and never how in general societies change and develop, how can we hope to engineer a better society? This is the topic of the next section.

SOCIAL ENGINEERING

Rational action

Any practical task involves the employment of some means to a given end. Acting rationally, or practical rationality as it is usually called, requires us, other things being equal, to choose the most efficient means to the end in view, that is, the means that is most likely to achieve the desired result at a minimum cost. So, for instance, someone who wants to get rid of a headache will normally find it cheapest, quickest and most effective to take aspirin. In doing so he or she will be choosing the most efficient means – taking aspirin – to a given end – relieving a headache.

This simple understanding of practical activity and the place of rationality within it is obviously incomplete, because it only tells us what makes the means to an end rational, not which ends it is rational for us to adopt. A full account of what it is to act rationally would also have to set up standards for rational ends as well as rational means. Nevertheless, even this simple conception can provide us with a useful test of the rationality of any proposed course of action, especially when the rationality of the desired end is not actually in question.

This is true of the present context. The result of the last seven chapters, if all the arguments have been sound, is a clearer conception of the sort of society it would be rational to aim at. To generate successful social policies, therefore, we now need to know what means to that end it would be rational to take, and the answer is – the most efficient means.

How do we know, in any given case, which means are efficient? How do we know that the steps we propose to take will bring about the effect we want? In most cases, our knowledge is based on personal experience and the shared experience of others, but in some it is based on abstract knowledge of causal connections. I may know from experience that 'Joe's' supplies the best pizzas, and hence that if I want a good pizza I should (if I am rational) go to 'Joe's'; or I may know a lot about about biochemistry and hence about the effects of nitrogen and potassium on certain cereals, and on the basis of this be able to recommend the best fertilizer. Strictly speaking, in neither case do I know what *will* produce the desired effect, only what is *most likely to*. But this knowledge of probabilities is enough for practical purposes, and enough to make my choice rational. To choose rationally is to choose the course of action most likely to produce the desired effect.

Most of us, most of the time, rely upon experience for knowledge of what is and what is not likely to be effective. The enormous advances that modern technology has made, however, arise from the systematic investigative approach of science. Here, as in other contexts, medicine provides one of the plainest examples. In the past doctors were obliged to rely upon their own experience of individual cases, together with something of the experience of others, and as result, though their services were often helpful and valued, they were severely restricted in the number of remedies at their disposal and, consequently, in the number of cures they could effect. The picture changed dramatically under the impact of medical science, the systematic investigation of the biology and chemistry of the human body. This science, by providing knowledge of cause and effect at an abstract but detailed level (at the level of cells and microbes rather than the level of fevers and fits), provided the possibility of devising remedies and cures far more effective than anything medicine had hitherto dreamed of.

A similar story might be repeated across a great deal of modern technology. Scientific investigation has replaced experience as the primary source of knowledge for technical means. This is not to suggest that personal practical experience could ever be wholly replaced by 'science': the use and adaptation of even the most advanced technology requires personal skill and experience. But it does suggest that where rigorous scientific investigation is possible, there is a corresponding possibility of advanced technology and hence of a much higher degree of control for individuals in the pursuit of their ends.

Another and no less striking example is chemical and electrical engineering. By investigating the properties of different materials at a molecular level, a huge new range of possibilities has opened up, and given modern engineering technologies which could not have been imagined as recently as seventy years ago.

Social technology

New technology is amongst the great benefits of modern science. It should be fairly obvious how the preceding paragraphs relate to the subject of this chapter. Throughout the book we have been concerned to delineate 'the good society', to discover the sort of society it would be most desirable to inhabit. If this is to be relevant to the practical tasks of political and social policy, what we have to do is to discover what means are most likely to produce the end at which we can now more clearly aim. This is a promising prospect if, as in medicine and engineering, we can avail ourselves of the results of appropriate scientific investigations. But if the arguments of the first section in this chapter are sound, this is precisely what we cannot do, since there is no social science to turn to. And if there is no social science, there can be no social technology.

To say that there is no social science is, of course, a claim rather stronger than the arguments of the last section strictly support. What we saw there is the possibility of a descriptive, empirical study of society which, especially given increasingly refined statistical techniques, will enable us to speak with greater confidence about existing social realities. But this sort of science, however valuable, is not enough to generate an appropriate technology. What we need is not descriptive analysis, but a theoretical understanding of social *causes*, and this is what we cannot have.

It is true that no argument has been given which shows conclusively that we cannot have this, only that as a matter of fact we do not have it. But the problem is that the reasons which best serve to explain the absence of any real theory in modern social science also suggest (though they do not prove) that there never will be any theory of the required sort. It is not that social scientists have not yet examined enough cases and are consequently short of data. Rather the problem is that they cannot legitimately universalize in the right way.

A simple but not inaccurate way of putting the same point is to say that whereas physical science has provided us with a great deal of knowledge about physical causes in general, and thus with the possibility of using that knowledge to bring about desired effects, virtually nothing is known about causality in the social world. Our knowledge of even the most highly intractable questions in medical science, such as the cause of cancer, is still far in advance of our knowledge of, for instance, the relation between poverty and crime. Indeed all we have in the way of a theoretical understanding of such things is some statistical correlations between different social phenomena whose interpretation remains uncertain.

One exception to this paucity of empirical social theory might be thought to be economics, in which mathematical models of great sophistication and complexity have been developed. Certainly it is true that in economics there are theories of a kind that have no counterpart in sociology. Moreover, politicians more readily aspire to the management of economies than they do to the engineering of whole societies.

The problem with these theories, however, is not their simplicity, but their application, and this brings us to the second major obstacle to social and economic engineering – the complexity of social systems.

The complexity of social systems

Let us suppose, for the sake of the argument, and contrary to my claims about the theoretical poverty of social science, that we are possessed of at least some advanced and sophisticated economic and social theories which could in principle be used in engineering a better society. There is still one advantage doctors have over aspiring social engineers, quite apart from the availability of a reliable body of relevant scientific knowledge, and that is the relative simplicity of the problems with which they have to deal. Although it is becoming fashionable to talk of medicine having to treat 'the whole person', it is nevertheless the case that for many physical ailments the specification of the problem, the prescription and application of a remedy, and the assessment of a cure are unambiguous. If I have a chest infection, this is probably fairly easy to detect and there may well be nothing obscure about its diagnosis. Similarly, the prescribing and taking of penicillin is a highly specific remedy, and the test for its effectiveness is clear. These things are never the case with social problems. Precisely what the problem is, what the cure is and whether it has been effective are always obscure and vexed questions.

For instance, 'unemployment' is usually thought of as a social and economic problem. Establishing that it really is a problem, however, is not simply a matter of computing figures. The reasons for someone's being unemployed are crucial. If there were an island of hereditary millionaires somewhere, *everyone* would be unemployed, but there would be no problem. In reality, the reasons for someone's being unemployed vary, and this variation makes it hard to determine just when unemployment is something to worry about and when it is not. Even where we are agreed that there is a good deal of involuntary and unwelcome unemployment, it is extremely difficult to say what policies might alter it, and as the figures change for better or worse it is difficult to tell what has caused them to change. In other words, every stage is beset by difficulty, the difficulty of defining the problem, devising a remedy and testing its effectiveness.

This is a feature of social and economic engineering of which we only need to be reminded, in fact, because it is made thoroughly familiar to us by the nature of political debates everywhere. These generally take the form of disagreements about whether there is a problem, and if so what it is, how it might be corrected and whether it has been corrected. That such debates continue after the 'experts' have given their opinions is not just a reflection of prejudice, rhetoric and ideological commitment among politicians (though there often is a measure of this), but of the hard fact that there is no incontestable way of settling these issues in anything like the way that problems in medicine, civil engineering, computer science and so on can be settled.

A large part of the reason for this is the sheer complexity of society. A policy initiated one year at the heart of government must, if it is to be applied at all, be carried out by a large number of individually minded people in the far reaches of government (and beyond) over a number of succeeding years. The implementation of even the clearest, most well-founded and best intentioned remedy for some social or economic ill will thus pass through a large number of stages, and at each stage unforeseen or novel circumstances will arise which call for interpretation of that policy and its adaptation to them. But this interpretation and adaptation cannot be supplied in advance by the initiating authority except in the form of the broadest guidelines, and this means that the control of the policy is removed further and further from the power and the intention of its original architect. Moreover, the more ambitious the policy, the greater the dispersion of control.

For instance, a government that wanted to disperse employment opportunities more widely throughout the country might have good reasons for thinking that regional economic aid policies were a sensible measure to take. But the implementation of those policies by officials takes place far from the centre of government, and crucially depends upon the response of those for whom the policies are intended. This means that the initiators of the policy do not have much control over its realization. Even when political leaders like Stalin have taken draconian measures to preserve their power and control down to the grass roots, they have been only partially successful.

Sometimes this is because the complexity of society shows itself in another way, the difficulty of foretelling the consequences of public policies with any degree of certainty. Regional aid policies provide another good example here. Whatever the intentions of their authors, however well based and well meant, individuals will see in them opportunities that others had not anticipated and, acting upon them, will bring about consequences that are quite unforeseen. Sometimes these unforeseen consequences are sufficient to thwart the very intentions of those who devised the policy. The European Common Agricultural Policy is perhaps one of the most outstanding examples of this.

For *any* social policy, then, the chances of its being applied and realized in a way that preserves the intention of its originators are fairly slim, and this means that it is only the most limited and piecemeal policies that stand much chance of success.

We can represent this conclusion quite generally in a mathematical form, in fact. Imagine a policy – call it P – which is meant to produce an effect E, and suppose at the same time that it must pass through at least five stages, a–e. Obviously the probability, given the successful completion of the first stage, that the second stage will be completed just as successfully will fall short of 1 (where 1 represents certainty of success and 0 certainty of failure). Given a as the first stage of P, then, the chance of b (the second stage) will be 0.7, let us say, and the chance of c given a and b also 0.7, and so on. To discover what the probability of E ever coming about is if we adopt P, we simply multiply the probabilities, and we find that the result is 0.1 – in other words, it is not likely to come about at all. What the mathematics shows is that as we increase the number of stages, the probability of success falls still further, so that even under the best conditions, the sheer complexity of society makes social engineering a highly uncertain undertaking.

Piecemeal engineering

Some people have thought that this argument implies that we can do nothing whatever in the way of social policy, and since this is obviously absurd, the argument must be flawed in some way. But in point of fact, all the figures do is to represent the truth that, in a complex system, the more complex your aim the less chance there is of its coming about. It does not show that in a complex system there is no chance of less ambitious schemes coming about. In other words there may still be scope for what Sir Karl Popper has called 'piecemeal engineering', as opposed to holistic engineering. So, for instance, assuming the truth of the conclusions of previous arguments, we might still reasonably hope to promote the right sort of equality by affirmative action programmes, we might succeed in shifting the emphasis from state to individual in the provision of health care, we might introduce more flexibility in age-limits, and we would certainly have good reason to resist moral censorship. What we would have no reason to do is engage in any ambitious scheme for restructuring society as a whole, and even if we act in the true spirit of piecemeal engineering we must acknowledge that one measure may well effectively undercut another, and that there is a good chance that any or all of them will be thwarted by unforeseen consequences and circumstances.

This is a rather important conclusion to have arrived at in a book on normative social philosophy, for of course the most ambitious plan we could possibly have is to engineer not just this or that society but 'the good society', and this now seems to be a ridiculously optimistic undertaking. But if so, what is the point of trying to discover what the good society is? What is the point of social philosophy? This is the subject of the next and final section.

SOCIAL PHILOSOPHY

A great deal of the interest and excitement in normative social philosophy arises from its being an attempt to see beyond the political problems of particular times and places and to discern clearly just what a good society would be like. And yet we have seen that any achievement of this sort is idle, since the best we can hope for is to engineer piecemeal improvements. There is no hope for the implementation of grand designs. Where, then, does this leave social philosophy?

The eighteenth-century writer and conversationalist, Dr Samuel Johnson, was once criticized for laughing at schemes for political improvement. In his defence he replied that such schemes are very laughable things, and with them the philosophy that lies behind them. But the philosophy of society is laughable in this sense only if we regard it as the beginning of a *scheme*, the foundation of some grand and imposing social blueprint. No doubt social theorizing has quite often been thought of in this way, but we are under no obligation to think of it like this and, given the arguments of this chapter, are more likely to discover its value if we do not. The point to grasp is that social philosophy may still have a *value* even if it does not have a use.

First, we can value the investigations of social philosophy, not because they tell us what to *do*, but because they tell us what to *think*. A detached concern with truth and understanding for their own sake is characteristic of all academic inquiry. This high-sounding ideal, however, need not be understood as a retreat into the ivory tower and away from the rough and tumble of the world outside. One of the great merits of social philosophy is that it can show us what we ought to think of the claims that political leaders and ordinary people make in the everyday world of public affairs and social policy, as well as the claims of the philosophers and theorists.

Secondly, social philosophy can tell us what it is reasonable to hope for and to support, even when there is no real prospect of controlling the social world sufficiently to have a major effect upon it. This is a feature it shares with moral philosophy in general. None of us is in a position to put an end to all the evils of this world, to trample down Satan under our feet, as older language has it, or to engineer sucessfully the triumph of good. But at least we can know what is good from what is evil, and we can thus be on the side of the angels, and hope for and speak for the right things. That we are able to do so as a result of philosophical thinking, if the claim about our relative powerlessness is true, makes philosophy more not less valuable than it otherwise might have been.

Thirdly, social philosophy can teach us to be critical, to demand reasons and explanations of ourselves and others, rather than rest content with the comforting rhetoric which

Suggestions for Further Reading

CHAPTER I   WHAT IS SOCIETY?

John Locke, *Second Treatise of Government*, ed. P. Laslett (Cambridge University Press, 1960), chs. 1–7.

Niccolo Machiavelli, *The Prince*, tr. George Bull (Penguin, Harmondsworth, 1961).

Karl Marx and Friedrich Engels, *The Communist Manifesto* (Penguin, Harmondsworth, 1967).

Robert Nozick, *Anarchy, State, and Utopia* (Basil Blackwell, Oxford, 1974), chs. 2–3.

Plato, *The Republic*, tr. H.D.P. Lee (Penguin, Harmondsworth, 1955).

R.H.Tawney, *Equality* (Allen and Unwin, London, 1964).

For a general critical survey of the principal social theorists of the past see:

John Plamenatz, *Man and Society*, 2 vols (Longman, London, 1963).

CHAPTER 2   SOCIETY AND THE INDIVIDUAL

David Hillel-Ruben, 'The Existence of Social Entities', *The Philosophical Quarterly* 32 (1982).

Steven Lukes, *Individualism* (Basil Blackwell, Oxford, 1973).

Anthony Quinton, 'Social Holism', *Proceedings of the Aristotelian Society* 1974–5.

CHAPTER 3   SOCIAL JUSTICE

Robert Nozick, *Anarchy, State, and Utopia* (Basil Blackwell, Oxford, 1974), ch. 7, section 1.

John Rawls, *A Theory of Justice* (Clarendon Press, Oxford, 1972), part 1, especially ch. 2.
Michael Walzer, *Spheres of Justice* (Martin Robertson, Oxford, 1983), ch. 1.

CHAPTER 4   SOCIAL EQUALITY AND AFFIRMATIVE ACTION

Ronald Dworkin, *A Matter of Principle* (Clarendon Press, Oxford, 1985), chs 8–9.
Ronald Dworkin, *Taking Rights Seriously* (Duckworth, London, 1977), ch. 9.
Michael Levin, 'Equality of Opportunity', *The Philosophical Quarterly* 31 (1981).
George Sher, 'Ancient Wrongs and Modern Rights', *Philosophy and Public Affairs* 10 (1981).
R.H. Tawney, *Equality* (Allen and Unwin, London, 1964), chs 4–5.
Bernard Williams, 'The Idea of Equality', in *Philosophy, Politics and Society*, eds P. Laslett and W.G. Runciman (Basil Blackwell, Oxford, 1962).

CHAPTER 5   HEALTH CARE PROVISION

Allen E. Buchanan, 'The Right to a Decent Minimum of Health Care', *Philosophy and Public Affairs* 13 (1984).
Norman Daniels, 'Health Care Needs and Distributive Justice', *Philosophy and Public Affairs* 10 (1981).
Michael Walzer, *Spheres of Justice* (Martin Robertson, Oxford, 1983), ch. 3.

CHAPTER 6   MORAL STANDARDS AND THE LAW

Patrick Devlin, *The Enforcement of Morals* (Oxford University Press, Oxford, 1965).
Ronald Dworkin, *Taking Rights Seriously* (Duckworth, London, 1977), ch. 10.
H.L.A. Hart, *Law, Liberty and Morality* (Oxford Univesity Press, Oxford, 1962).
J.S. Mill, 'On Liberty', in *Three Essays* (Oxford University Press, Oxford, 1975).

CHAPTER 7   CHILDREN IN SOCIETY

Patrick Gardiner, 'Liberty and Compulsory Education', in *Of Liberty*, ed. A. Phillips Griffiths (Cambridge University Press, Cambridge, 1982).

Amy Gutman, 'What's the use of going to school?', in *Utilitarianism and Beyond*, ed. A. Sen and B. Williams (Cambridge University Press, Cambridge, 1982).

John Harris, 'The Political Status of Children', in *Contemporary Political Philosophy*, ed. Keith Graham (Cambridge University Press, Cambridge, 1981).

Hugh LaFollette, 'Licensing Parents', *Philosophy and Public Affairs*, (1979–80).

CHAPTER 8   ENGINEERING THE GOOD SOCIETY

Alastair MacIntyre, 'Is a Science of Comparative Politics Possible?', in *Against the Self-Images of the Age* (Duckworth, London, 1971).

Karl Popper, *The Poverty of Historicism*, 3rd edn (Routledge and Kegan Paul, London, 1961).

Rush Rhees, 'Social Engineering', in *Without Answers* (Routledge and Kegan Paul, London, 1969).

Index